Active History in Key Stages 3 and 4

ALAN FARMER AND PETER KNIGHT

David Fulton Publish
London

David Fulton Publishers Ltd
2 Barbon Close, London WC1N 3JX

First published in Great Britain by
David Fulton Publishers 1995

Note: The right of Alan Farmer and Peter Knight to be identified as the authors of this work has been asserted by them in accordance with the Copyright, Designs and Patents Act 1988.

British Library Cataloguing in Publication Data

A catalogue record for this book is available from the British Library

ISBN 1-85346-305-1

Typeset by Textype Typesetters, Cambridge
Printed in Great Britain by the Cromwell Press, Melksham

Contents

Series Editor's Foreword

History as a subject taught in primary and secondary schools has changed considerably since the end of the Second World War – and particularly since the 1970s. At the secondary level, the consensus that once existed has been replaced by a fierce debate about the nature and purposes of school history – a debate that has been given added focus by the arrival of the National Curriculum. The agenda for this debate is invariably about content, its function and its relation to skills. Put crudely, should the study of history move from the acquisition of 'considerable and diverse knowledge' to a greater emphasis on skills and conceptual understanding?

Right at the outset, the authors of this useful and practical guide to successful history teaching nail their colours to the 'content mast', arguing further that it is vital that this content is understood and has meaning for all those studying the subject at school. Indeed, the emphasis throughout the book is on *active* learning, learning characterised by mental liveliness which is itself stimulated by effective classroom teaching. For the two authors, motivating pupils is at the very heart of the teaching and learning process. At the same time, good quality work is seen to depend on history teachers possessing a *principled* view of the nature of their subject and its various purposes. Only then can pupils be presented with the sort of activities and tasks that will give them a positive and enthusiastic view of the subject.

Clyde Chitty
Birmingham
December 1994

Introduction

The nature of school history

This is not the easiest time to write a book on school history, when a new National Curriculum is emerging, with all its attendant uncertainties. However, there has been no good time over the past decade to write anything like the definitive book on this topic. As we will show in Chapter 1, this – and arguably the last five decades too – has been a time of uncertainty and upheaval. We are told that we now face five years without change but we rather doubt that it will be the case.

Now seems to be as good a time as any to take stock. Although some of our assumptions about the future may prove to be inaccurate, this is not disastrous because our main assumption is that it is possible to say a lot about good teaching and learning in history, more or less regardless of what a National Curriculum says.

While learning and teaching history is our focus, we think that we ought to say something about what we see as the main justification for teaching history. This means saying something about the relative importance of 'skills' and content, an issue that has divided history teachers in the late 20th century.

The debate goes back to classical times. For the Greeks, the word history meant 'inquiry'. For the Romans it meant, 'things that had been done'. If we have to decide, we probably prefer the Roman (content) to the Greek (skill) definition. The best justification for history in our view is that it is the memory of society. Some memories are more important than others and should be transmitted to the next generation. Historical 'skills' – and we are not sure we like that word – are a means to an end, not the end itself. Children will not understand history unless they acquire considerable and diverse knowledge. Education is crucially tied up with knowledge and being educated means, crudely, knowing a lot.

It follows that we are not against the notion of a National Curriculum in history. Some types of human experience are more important and significant to us than others and ought to be taught. Different content carries with it different messages about a society's cultural identity, and since there is always argument about what that cultural identity is, choice of content cannot be dispassionate, as the continuing arguments about the content of the National Curriculum for history have shown. We will not join this debate, since our concern here is more with teaching and learning methods. However, we do argue in Chapter 6 that school history has much to contribute to important themes in the curriculum as a whole and that a historical perspective ought to be brought to bear on important issues, such as inter-cultural understanding, environmental education and personal and social education.

Having nailed our colours to the *content* mast, we stress in Chapter 2 that there is a need for three masts. Content, by itself, is not enough. It is vital that this historical knowledge is understood and has meaning for each learner, which implies that they develop an awareness of the *concepts* used in the study of history. This, in turn, implies that they need to have a good grasp of the *procedures* (or 'skills', if you wish) used in history and of the *purposes* of the study.

Active history

Active learning is invariably seen by the educational intelligentsia as 'a good thing'. John Fines, for example, thought that 'good learning is always active learning' (cit. Bourdillon, 1994, p.125). In his view active learning in history is when children rather than the teacher do the work. It is connected with children working with problems of evidence which he sees as 'challenging, mind-stretching, satisfying' and which helps them 'make sense of what is being studied'.

We do not entirely accept this rather tight definition. All learning is 'active' and good quality learning is undoubtedly active. We suspect we have a far more eclectic view of what constitutes 'active' learning in history than Fines, stressing that in our view anything which is effective is 'active'.

Active learning by the pupils cannot be divorced from active teaching. Active teaching is teaching that encourages learners to take a *mentally* active stance to the history material that they encounter. In Chapter 3 we suggest a number of techniques for doing this and in Chapter 4 we develop them through a review of four history units, two of which are Key Stage 3 (KS3) units and two of which also belong to that stage but are also popular GCSE courses.

We have no doubts that the history teacher remains the most important – and most expensive – resource in any classroom situation. Teachers decide which methods and resources to use. Their general enthusiasm and oral contributions are a basic but vital stimulus to learning. Moreover, they have considerable influence – even in the National Curriculum age – over what is taught in the classroom. Individual teachers' interests, expertise and enthusiasms do and should play an important part in determining what is taught. Interest is often caught in the company of other people and the real enthusiast can have a truly infectious effect. Motivating pupils is at the very heart of the teaching and learning process. If a teacher can foster a positive and enthusiastic approach to history, that teacher is succeeding. We claim that the techniques and approaches that we review have considerable power to motivate learners and to encourage a positive and enthusiastic view of history.

Of course, if assessment techniques are out of kilter with teaching methods, then the dissonance is likely to work against good quality learning, a point we elaborate in Chapter 5.

This, then, is our view of good quality history learning: learning characterised by mental liveliness, encouraged by purposeful and flexible teaching.

QUALITY IN SECONDARY SCHOOLS AND COLLEGES SERIES

Series Editor, Clyde Chitty

This new series publishes on a wide range of topics related to successful education for the 11-19 age group. It reflects the growing interest in whole-school curriculum planning, together with the effective teaching of individual subjects and themes. There will also be books devoted to management and administration, examinations and assessment, pastoral care strategies, relationships with parents and governors and the implications for schools of changes in teacher education.

Early titles include:

Managing the Learning of History
Richard Brown
1-85346-345-0

English and the OFSTED Experience
Bob Bibby and Barrie Wade
1-85346-357-4

English as a Creative Art: Literary Concepts Linked to Creative Writing
Linden Peach and Angela Burton
1-85346-368-X

Geography 11-16: Rekindling Good Practice
Bill Marsden
1-85346-296-9

Learning to Teach: a Guide for School-Based Initial and In-Service Training
Julian Stern
1-85346-371-X

The Literate Imagination: Renewing the Secondary English Curriculum
Bernard T. Harrison
1-85346-300-0

Making Sense of English: the National Curriculum
Roger Knight
1-85346-374-4

Moral Education through English 11-16
Ros McCulloch and Margaret Mathieson
1-85346-276-4

Partnership in Secondary Initial Teacher Education
Edited by Anne Williams
1-85346-361-2

Heeding Heads: Secondary Heads and Educational Commentators in Dialogue
Edited by David Hustler, Tim Brighouse and Jean Rudduck
1-85346-358-2

CHAPTER 1

A Recent History of History Teaching

Most historians tend to believe that the best way to understand the present and forecast the future is to know something (and preferably a lot!) about the past. We are certainly convinced that any meaningful understanding of the present history teaching situation in school requires a historical perspective. It should be said that there have existed strongly held and divergent opinions about history teaching over the last half century. In consequence, the debate about history teaching has been lively and contentious. We shall attempt to tell the truth as we see it – but we are aware that there are many truths.

Our purpose is not simply one of historical propriety. Through showing how views of what counts as good quality school history have changed, we shall show how complex a task it is to produce a good school history curriculum. We shall also be showing ways in which good history is active history – demanding active imaginations, active thinking and active, purposeful teaching.

Old history

There is undoubtedly a stereotypical view of what history teaching was like four or five decades ago. Old history teaching is usually characterised as being a received subject: passive pupils were fed facts of British (with some European) history; chalk and talk dominated with little discussion of sources. Unstead is often depicted as a symbolic representative of old history. He produced a number of best-selling textbooks which followed a chronological approach, were full of artists' impressions, and contained little in the way of primary sources. 'A great part of the understanding of the teaching of history', he argued, 'consists of imparting information and facts to children and the best source of information is still their teacher.' (1956, pp. 49–50). History, thought Unstead, is a sequence, a stream of events, a continuous story, and it is folly to present it as anything else. Additionally, history should teach moral values.

Supporters of the so-called 'new' history in the 1970s invariably con-demned old history in the way that those who perceive themselves to be revolutionaries tend to criticise the past. Many of these criticisms – which have stuck – were, unfortunately, simplistic and distorted, with the result that much of the more recent curriculum debate about history has taken place, as Aldrich pointed out, in 'an ahistorical and unhistorical context' (1984, p. 210). Actually reading the books on history teaching published in the 1950s gives one a very different picture of the age. In 1950, for example, The Association of Assistant Masters in Secondary Schools pro-duced an influential text about teaching history. This book was generally optimistic about the future of teaching the past. 'Many more specialist his-torians are teaching History in the schools.' the authors noted. 'Their approach to their subject is more philosophical and they ask their pupils more often for reflections upon what they learn, rather than for knowledge alone.' (AAM, 1950, pp. xiii–xiv). The book stressed the need for enquiry methods, praised the use of sources, and condemned the practice of teach-ing history as a simple body of received fact. Even Unstead, so often regarded as epitomising old history, expressed the view that history has the power to enrich the mind and imagination of children (1956, p. 2) – a sen-timent which most history teachers then and now would probably rally around.

It may well have been the case, of course, that much chalk-face history teaching fell short of these high ideals. However, it was wrong of the new history disciples to condemn old history as all bad, thereby damning many dedicated and inspiring teachers. History teachers before the 1960s were limited by the technology available and often had little alternative but to rely on chalk and talk. What is often forgotten is that many teachers of this generation were remarkably skilled in both media. The oral approach has the great advantage of transferring the enthusiasm of a teacher to a class more quickly than any other method. Many old history teachers succeeded (with the help of their subject) in winning the interest of many children – including us.

Moreover, some reasonable textbooks were produced – not least by Unstead! His emphasis on the visual dimension was of fundamental importance. His simple language and his ability to simplify very difficult concepts is often forgotten.

Nor was old history all chalk, talk and textbook. From the early decades of the 20th century, history pundits had stressed the importance of using primary sources in teaching, and throughout the 1950s hordes of enthusi-astic history teachers did their best to bring source material into the class-room. Sometimes they had no option but to read sources – *They saw it Happen* was a particularly successful series, containing a wealth of often vivid eyewitness accounts. By 1960 it was possible to obtain reasonably cheap facsimiles of original documents for classroom use. (Batho's *Archive Teaching Units* were put together at Sheffield University in 1957: the first *Jackdaw* packs appeared in 1964). Many teachers took pupils to historical sites, where possible hired film, used slides and filmstrips, and realised the importance of artefacts. A patch approach – examining a few periods in some depth – was a common feature of many school history courses, and favoured by the experts. Local history also had its supporters.

At the start of the 1960s history seemed to be in a strong position. It was regarded as an important area of academic enquiry and was a major examination subject, being the sixth most popular subject at O level and the fourth most popular at A level in 1966 – far more popular than in the 1990s! Many pupils found it a rewarding activity, even if they could not always see its usefulness. Interest then, as now, in part reflected the subject matter and in part reflected good history teaching.

History in danger?

As the 1960s progressed, however, there was increasing unease about the place of history in the school curriculum. In a 1968 article entitled 'History in Danger', Mary Price concluded that history was losing out as a subject in its own right and was threatened by social studies and integrated humanities (Price, 1968). Booth's *History Betrayed* (1969) was a more root and branch attack on the teaching of history. Booth's surveys convinced him that many pupils were bored with history which they saw as irrelevant to their needs and interests. He was particularly critical of the fact that learners were not active in history lessons and were often simply taught to regurgitate facts.

Given the dangers, innovators claimed that there was a need for a solid theoretical basis for rethinking school history. Some historians sought to extend their professionalism by seeking illumination from different disciplines. The ideas of Piaget (a genetic epistemologist interested in children's conceptual development), Bloom (who emphasised the importance of isolating and developing specific educational objectives), Bruner (who stressed the need to define the essentials of subjects in order to provide direction and coherence, along with the notion of spiralling to reinforce and develop the main procedures/concepts) and Plowden (who stressed activity in learning and the need to 'know how' rather than to 'know that') were soon to have a massive impact on school history. Interestingly, none of these educationalists was primarily concerned with history or actually knew very much about teaching history!

Place, Time and Society 8–13 Project

At the start of the 1970s two Schools Council curriculum initiatives affected thinking and practice in school history. The first was *Place, Time and Society 8–13*. This Project, set up in 1971, aimed to define some common principles for planning and organising work not just for history but for geography and social science subjects in the middle years of schooling. The Project team made the valid point that in most primary schools there was little evidence of a systematic approach to the selection of content and little emphasis on progression in learning skills. Themes were frequently taught at the whim of a teacher and usually little thought was given to *overall* schemes of work.

The Project commended a systematic approach to choosing the content, skills and concepts to be promoted in schools, concluding that teachers involved in the process of curriculum planning for history, geography and social studies should consider seven key concepts: values and beliefs; similarity and difference; power; communication; continuity and change; conflict/consensus; causes and consequences.

The specific history concepts highlighted by the Project were to resurface again and again over the next two decades – continuity and change, cause and effect, and similarity and difference. The Project also introduced the history world to the notion of empathy.

The Schools Council Project, History 13–16

Far more significant than *Place, Time and Society* was the *Schools Council Project, History 13–16* (later known as the *Schools History Project* or SHP). Established in 1972, it was the first *national* curriculum programme devoted exclusively to history. Arising as a result of concern over the erosion of the position of history in schools, one of its key aims was to counter the perceived integrationist/social science threat. It claimed that history, with its own distinctive approach to human affairs, had a unique role to play in the education of the young. This role emphasised people as individuals, rather than as sociological data or geographical phenomena.

By 1976 SHP had developed an entire course based upon two pillars: the belief that school history should reflect both adolescents' personal and social needs and the nature of the subject. The Project also depicted history as a process of enquiry instead of just received knowledge. It favoured pupils working investigatively with sources, asking the same questions as professional historians. Its main concerns were to promote

● evaluation and interpretation of sources;

- empathetic reconstruction of the ways of thinking and feeling of people of a different time or place;
- analysis of causation and motivation.

Unlike *Place, Time and Society*, SHP produced exemplary materials for pupils and teachers. These came in two forms. For 13–14 year olds (Y9), there was a set of *What is History?* materials which aimed to introduce them to ideas about the nature of history and to some of the skills they would need to use when studying it. Conceived as a one term course, the *What is History?* package consisted of the following:

1. People in the past – an introduction to the content of history and to chronology;
2. History as detective work;
3. Looking at evidence – an introduction to the variety of historical evidence;
4. Problems of evidence;
5. Asking questions – an introduction to causation and motivation in history.

The examination syllabus for 14–16 year olds developed ideas introduced in the *What is History?* unit. It aimed to help adolescents

- understand their present world;
- understand people of a different time;
- understand how change occurs in human affairs;
- develop leisure interests in the historical environment.

There were four modules:

1. A study of an aspect of modern world history, such as The Rise of Communist China, The Move to European Unity, or The Irish Question;
2. A study in depth, for example Elizabethan England, Britain 1815–51, or the American West 1840–90;
3. A study in Development through time (students initially studied Medicine);
4. A study of the history around us, for example Prehistoric Britain, Roman Britain, Castles and Fortified Houses, Studies in the Making of the Rural Landscape, Town Development, Industrial Archaeology.

The SHP examination was pioneering in three ways:

- It had a considerable coursework element (including fieldwork), with a 40% weighting. This was not a means of rewarding conscientious students who produced bulky, neat projects. Nor was it a method of compensating pupils who were likely to fail to achieve good results in an exam. Its main *raison d'être* was that it was the most effective method of assessing many of the objectives of the course.

- The second of the examination papers was based on unseen evidence, reflecting SHP's philosophy that the historical skills of using sources were important and ought to be realistically assessed.
- Structured questions were set instead of essays (used at GCE) or multiple-choice items (used at CSE). They were linked to tight assessment objectives.

SHP provided a coherent case for history, visible to pupils, history teachers and colleagues alike. It was well-supported with materials and provided assessment which did more than simply ask pupils to regurgitate facts. Pupils covered a variety of topics and approaches which arguably provided a broader understanding of the wares history had to offer than a two year course devoted solely to Modern World or British Social and Economic history. SHP made learners study a lot of historical content but it was the stress on source-based skills which most history teachers came to associate with SHP. It became tagged as 'the evidence approach'.

The evaluation study (Shemilt, 1980) indicated that high- and average-ability pupils following SHP developed more sophisticated concepts of historical causation and development, a clearer understanding of the nature and use of evidence, and a far sharper awareness of the historical form of knowledge than pupils who had not followed SHP. (Cynics claimed that children who had taught using SHP *should* have a better grasp of the SHP way than pupils who hadn't!).

SHP continued to develop, refining assessment techniques, developing new materials and providing INSET for teachers throughout Britain. By the early 1980s it had become politically correct, many of those involved with SHP in its early days going on to win powerful places in the inspectorate or advisory services. Not to do SHP was to be seen as reactionary. SHP disciples believed that the Project was the only method of teaching school history and by 1990 about one third of GCSE history entries were for the SHP course.

New history

In many respects the 1970s and 1980s were exciting times in history teaching. The new emphasis on the skills/concept approach seemed to offer a language for lesson planning and a more precise tool for assessment purposes, while the evidence approach made history seem to be a physically active study, through fieldwork and work with artefacts, as well as a mentally active study.

There were also major practical developments. The photocopier came into its own, allowing teachers to produce better worksheets and provide children with a variety of written and visual sources. Most schools and many teachers acquired video recorders with the result that a colossal amount of film material was potentially available in the classroom. There was increased emphasis on simulation techniques and the computer made its appearance. History textbooks improved considerably with more emphasis on the visual dimension. The easily photocopiable two page spread per topic, containing a variety of sources and sometimes well-conceived tasks, became the norm, although we wonder whether this has been an unmixed blessing.

The teaching profession now talked about new history. This meant different things to different people but an emphasis on source-based work was generally regarded as the principal foundation of the new history. Nor was there any doubt that SHP was new history's corner-stone.

Opposition to new history

However, not all teachers were convinced by the new history in general and by SHP in particular. Practical reservations were:

- SHP materials were costly – so much so that some claimed that it was a monopolistic publisher's plot.
- Materials were not geared to the needs of children of below average achievements.
- Arguably the Project encouraged a didactic style of teaching with an over-dependence on set – straitjacket – texts and many SHP exam students tended to regurgitate model answers not underpinned by a solid grasp of the concept involved (SUJB, 1984). SHP lessons could easily become a rush through source material, and source-based tasks a worse tyranny than the tyranny of chalk and talk.

Active history had been promised but, fieldwork notwithstanding, it had not always materialised.

Others had theoretical reservations:

- Many were critical of the emphasis which SHP seemingly placed on skills and concepts rather than on actual content. Some SHP advocates did seem to suggest that the study of manhole covers in Wigan was as valid as study of the causes of World War 2. Critics responded that there is more to history than detective work on sources and if this was all there was to history, pupils might as well study Arthur Conan Doyle and Agatha Christie. The methodology of history, they said, should not be all-important: content matters.

- The segmented approach of SHP presented pupils with a mélange of Arab-Israeli politics, Egyptian medics and Elizabethan clerics. This, critics claimed, compared poorly to a coherent and sustained attempt to grasp the collapse of European World hegemony.

Some were concerned about new history's seeming fetish for primary sources. Burston and Thompson (1967) had pointed out that children had difficulty in coping with primary sources which were not innately interesting, enjoyable, or even understandable. Dickinson and Lee (1978) stressed the importance of secondary sources which provide the framework of history as a public form of knowledge. No historian would embark on any subject without having the sense and courtesy to read what colleagues past and present are saying/have said. They emphasised the fact that primary sources are useless unless pupils have some idea of the context and are thus in a position to ask questions about the sources.

Even Bruner's notion that pupils should do what real historians do, was challenged. Watts (1972) developed an interesting analogy which shook, if it did not altogether topple, Bruner's spiral curriculum model. He claimed that there are historical producers, consumers and merchants. The producers professionally devote themselves to discovering, validating and presenting historical material. Consumers have a response or experience from an encounter with historical material. Between the two lies the class of historical merchants whose business is to stimulate demand by showing people what a historical experience can be and to find ways of presenting the sometimes dreary products of the professional historian to a wider public. Producer, merchant and consumer have different but equally reputable ways of handling historical material. The house rules of production ought not to dictate the nature of the other two processes which have their own characteristics and status. In other words history teachers should not try to define a historical education primarily in terms of an apprenticeship to professional historians. Classroom activities do not have to be made into simplified versions of professional techniques.

By the early 1980s the history teaching fraternity was split. Some favoured a skills/concepts-based approach – although there was some debate about which precise skills and concepts. Others supported a content-based approach, stressing that skills were simply a means to an end. Moreover, there were very different opinions about the nature of the content that should be taught. Those on the 'left' tended to favour the underside of history: they were less concerned with British history and more inclined to support women's history or claim that attention should be focused on the background of newcomers to Britain. The 'right' tended to favour conventional British history.

Growing consensus

Sir Keith Joseph helped the move to consensus. In an almost unprecedented speech in February 1984 (Education Secretaries had rarely spoken in defence of a particular subject), he attacked the accumulation of unrelated facts and stressed the importance of understanding and skills (Joseph, 1984). But children, he claimed, could not and should not do precisely what professional historians do. Content was important, and some bits of content were more important than others, and a syllabus of source material alone was not enough – history should provide a chronological map for pupils and British history was especially important. There was a need for well-informed, thoughtful citizens, accustomed to weighing evidence and forming their own conclusions. Good history teaching could help satisfy this need.

The HMI blue book, *History in the Primary and Secondary Years* (DES, 1985) also assisted the move towards consensus. HMI accepted that pupils needed to know both 'how' and 'what' and argued that there was no fundamental conflict of interest between content and skills: both were equally important. Content-based courses could and should be taught using pupil-centred activity and problem-solving, source-based methods.

HMI went on to express concern about progression in history teaching, claiming that primary children often did very similar tasks to 16 year olds. They argued there was a need for greater clarity of thought on the learning objectives that should underpin good classroom history and also a need for a range of structured, diverse and open-ended classroom activities which needed to be monitored. Without such monitoring, they said, progression could not be established and measured. HMI stressed the need for a strategic view of the history curriculum across primary and secondary years in order to ensure a broad thrust of progression as pupils got older. This broad planning for progression was exemplified by a diagram that suggested age-related objectives for pupil progress in historical skills (1985, pp.18–19).

Hard on the blue book's heels came GCSE. This required students to

- recall, evaluate and select knowledge relevant to the context and to deploy it in a clear and coherent form;
- make use of and understand the concepts of cause and consequence, continuity and change, similarity and difference;
- show an ability to look at events and issues from the perspective of people in the past;
- show the skills necessary to study a wide variety of historical evidence which should include both primary and secondary written sources, statistical and visual material, artefacts, text books and orally transmitted information

- by comprehending and extracting information from it;
- by interpreting and evaluating it – distinguishing between fact, opinion and judgement; pointing to deficiencies (e.g. gaps and inconsistencies) in the material as evidence; detecting bias;
- by comparing various types of historical evidence, reach conclusions based on this comparison.

For some these objectives (which were to a large extent based on SHP practice) seemed to presage a fundamental change in the way history would be assessed and taught in schools.

GCSE wanted to give all pupils a chance to show what they knew, understood and could do. However, neither GCSE general criteria nor subject-specific criteria for history laid down precisely how students should be assessed. This was left to examination groups who, in the event, all decided that there should be a common paper and common questions for all pupils, irrespective of ability. Grades were to be determined by the quality of pupil responses to open-ended questions. Examiners described this as differentiation by outcome – as opposed to differentiation by task (i.e. setting different questions for pupils of different ability). An important concomitant of differentiation by outcome was a 'levels of response' mark-scheme. GCSE examiners established a number of possible responses to a question and arranged them in hierarchical levels according to their conceptual complexity. Thus pupils might be given a causation question asking why a particular event happened. Monocausal answers got low marks whereas high marks were given for answers describing a web of causation.

Conscientious teachers, keen to familiarise their pupils with the sort of question that they would meet in their examinations, began to apply levels of response marking to lower secondary classes. But differentiation by outcome was not without its critics. Some felt that an exclusive reliance on common questions often created language difficulties for weaker pupils while limiting the amount of challenge that was available for higher-attaining pupils. Some also questioned the validity of the conceptual hierarchies that underpinned levels of response mark-schemes. There was, too, a general fear that history had been atomised into its constituent parts, simply for assessment purposes, and that the assessment tail would end up wagging the history dog.

On the other hand, schools were able to keep on teaching the popular Modern World History and British Social and Economic History courses and students still had to learn a fair amount of information. Thus the compromise which Sir Keith Joseph and HMI had hoped for – the linkage of content and skills – seemed to have been realised. Only a few teachers were prepared to be guillotined in defence of the *ancien régime*.

But empathy *did* become an issue. Empathy had crept into common history usage in the 1970s. Before this historians had tended to use Collingwood's notion of vicarious imagination when trying to explain the important historical skill (?) of trying to get into someone's mind (e.g. Caesar's as he crossed the Rubicon) so as to understand why people in the past thought and acted as they did (Collingwood, 1946). The idea of utilising children's imagination in history was hardly new. For generations teachers had asked children to write imaginary logs, plan imaginary newspapers, design imaginary posters and write imaginary letters.

SHP, however, made empathy respectable: it appeared in every part of the SHP's work. By the mid 1980s empathetic understanding had come to be regarded as one of history's distinctive traits, helping to justify its place in the core curriculum. History HMI in 1985 had no doubts about its importance. They were convinced that pupils of all ages and abilities should be encouraged to empathise – whether by discussion, simulations, roleplay or drama.

With the coming of GCSE, empathy was now a specific objective which needed to be assessed. Was this actually possible? The real guru on historical empathy was Shemilt (1984). He thought that at a basic level children often held a patronising attitude to people in the past. They tended to believe that people acted as they did because they were stupid!/earlier than us/not as developed. Children at the next level were able to put themselves into the shoes of people in the past, but tended to apply 20th century motives, attitudes, feelings and values when explaining their behaviour. At a higher level, students understood that people in the past held different values but tended to assume that all people in Tudor times had one – Tudor – view. Students at the highest level of empathetic conceptualisation appreciated that different people at different times had different views which were only accessible to historians through sources.

Shemilt believed that many of the exercises commonly conceived under the name of empathy too easily degenerated into recitations of mere narrative. His ideal empathy tasks were structured assignments asking pupils to explain why people acted or thought as they did. Shemilt's ideas were made generally accessible to teachers in a SREB booklet, *Empathy in History* (1986). For several years history teachers talked knowledgeably about everyday, stereotyped and differentiated historical empathy. But not all were convinced. There had always been some who argued that children, almost by definition, were unable to empathise meaningfully with adults, although most history teachers seem to have been of the (common sense) view that most children of secondary age can empathise with all kinds of people. The fiercest critics of historical empathy, however, did not necessarily believe that pupils could not empathise: instead they were critical of the way that empathy was being assessed and suspected that it could not be meaningfully assessed. Ann Low-Beer, for example, criticised the empathetic questions set in exams and condemned Shemilt's crude conceptual framework (TES, 10.4.87). Empathy, in her opinion, was an essentially elusive concept, a feeling as much as a skill, and certainly unexaminable.

While most history teachers were probably a bit cynical about Shemilt's levels, they seemed to accept that one of their most important tasks was to get children to think about and try to understand why people in the past acted and lived as they did. They were told that empathy had to be assessed and Shemilt provided a useful (albeit simplistic and/or flawed) model for measuring children's empathetic understanding.

On the eve of the National Curriculum

Despite the debates on empathy, GCSE was generally seen as a good thing and by 1990 there were relatively few problems with the 14–16 age range. However the 11–14 situation was different. There was no guarantee that pupils would study any meaningful history before the age of 14. Certainly the history that was taught varied in quality, quantity and organisation. In some schools history was taught in splendid isolation. In others it was integrated – but integration meant very different things in different schools. The result was that a great deal was left to chance. To make matters worse, liaison between primary and secondary schools with regard to history teaching was rare. It was thus possible for pupils to study historical topics two or three times. Most secondary school history departments, assuming that no meaningful history work was done at primary schools, started new intakes with a *What is History?* unit! Critics could point to the fact that history was a declining subject. By 1990 fewer than 50% of pupils opted to take history beyond 14.

Yet, it is possible to be more positive about the state of history immediately prior to the National Curriculum. Many of the ideas of GCSE were rubbing off on lower school teaching and most teachers enjoyed the freedom prevalent in teaching lower school groups. Research by Patrick (1988) and Spartacus Publishers (1988) indicated that something akin to a National Curriculum was already in place in most secondary schools. After an initial *'What is History?'* unit, most schools focused on British history and, starting with the Romans, headed chronologically forwards. There were some interesting attempts to widen the content of school history, in particular developments in women's history and black history. Textbooks and topic books were published to support these new initiatives.

The National Curriculum

The National Curriculum was designed to ensure that pupils got less of a 'lucky dip' curriculum and that there was a rational structure for continuity and progression. In 1989 the History Working Group (HWG) was set up and told to assume that all pupils from the ages of 5–16 would study history. Normally the equivalent of 3–4 periods of a 40 period week would be available for history for Key Stages 1–3.

The HWG issued an interim report in April 1990 and its final report in July 1990. Although many of the recommendations of the (far from final) report were to be disregarded, the HWG's justification for history and for its own proposals is essential reading for anyone interested in history teaching.

The HWG cleverly steered between the Scylla of skills and the Charybdis of content. It stated that in order to have integrity, the study of history must be grounded in a thorough knowledge of the past; must employ rigorous historical method; and must involve a range of interpretations and explanations. Together these elements make an organic whole; if any one of them is missing the outcome is not history. The content of the National Curriculum was to be delivered by Programmes of Study (PoS). The skills were to be the basis of the Attainment Targets (ATs). In this way the HWG hoped to ensure that the teaching of history was not characterised by undisciplined use of the imagination, nor by exercises designed to develop skills in isolation from a solid foundation of historical information, nor by the mere acquisition of quantities of historical information that contribute little, if anything, to an enduring understanding of the past.

The Government, aware that history was the most political of all the National Curriculum subjects, doubted whether the HWG's approach put sufficient emphasis on pupils acquiring historical knowledge. The HWG, therefore, was asked to review its proposals with a view to including essential historical knowledge in the ATs. But the HWG stuck to its guns and made a strong case for not having a knowledge AT or including information within the Statement of Attainments (SoAs). It saw no way of assessing knowledge except by accumulation: that is, a level 1 pupil should know ten facts, a level 2 pupil 20 facts, etc. Unfortunately, someone knowing 100 facts may have a worse understanding than someone who can recall 50 facts! Moreover, it is hard to argue that one piece of historical knowledge is somehow more difficult than another. There are no grounds for suggesting that The Battle of Hastings is an easier fact than The Spanish Armada. The HWG concluded that the only practical way to ensure that historical knowledge was taught, learned and assessed, was by clearly spelling out the essential content in the PoS, and assessing that content through the skills-based ATs. The Geography Working Group, in contrast, proposed content-led ATs, an approach that was to prove quite unworkable.

After a brief flirtation with four ATs, and after another national consultation, the Statutory Orders for history finally settled on three:

AT1: Knowledge and understanding of history

This was renamed by John MacGregor, the Education Secretary, to make the National Curriculum more acceptable to those who wanted to have a content-led AT. In substance, however, the AT was concerned with children's understanding of key concepts. It had three strands:

1. change and continuity
2. causes and consequence
3. knowing and understanding key features of past situations.

AT2: Interpretations of history

AT3: The use of historical sources

Notice that there was no mention of empathy – although empathetic understanding was implicit in AT1.

The PoS were a means of achieving the ATs. The HWG was concerned that the National Curriculum should provide breadth and thus insisted that teachers should teach political, economic, social and cultural history. It was also concerned with balance, requiring study of a range of periods – ancient, medieval and modern British history. There were eight PoS at Key Stage 3. Five of these were core :

- The Roman Empire
- Medieval realms: Britain 1066–1500
- The making of the United Kingdom: crowns, parliaments and peoples 1500–1750
- Expansion, trade and industry: Britain 1750–1900
- The era of the Second World War.

These units had to be taught (with the exception of The Roman Empire) in chronological order on the grounds that chronology provides a mental framework or map which gives coherence to the study of history.

There were three supplementary study units – a British, a European and a non-European unit – and teachers could design their own units if they saw fit. School-designed units were subject to definite ground rules but did allow teachers to draw on their own professional skills, knowledge and enthusiasm.

The simultaneous issue of Orders for Wales and Northern Ireland confirmed the governmental view that through history pupils should acquire first and foremost a knowledge of their country's past.

The impact of the National Curriculum

In many respects the National Curriculum was a tremendous success. It certainly strengthened the place of history in the primary curriculum and increased its status and its position as a separate subject at Key Stage 3. In some schools it resulted in more time being allocated to history, although few schools allocated more than 7% of curriculum time to history. The linkage of content and skills satisfied both traditionalists and progressives. The content at Key Stage 3 was generally seen to be appropriate and was certainly not totally new – at least as far as most secondary school history teachers were concerned. There remained considerable room for teachers to determine their own approaches and ways of delivering the PoS; nor were the ATs totally new or unmanageable. The links with GCSE were many and obvious.

However, it was clear from the start that there were problems with the National Curriculum. Most teachers thought there were too many study units and too much content in some units (especially *The making of the UK* and *Expansion, trade and industry*). The result was teachers racing like demented jockeys in an attempt to complete a never-ending syllabus race. There was also a general feeling that the content of some units (e.g. *The making of the UK*) was too demanding for many pupils and there was particular concern that the content of the Key Stage 4 programme was dull and unlikely to motivate 14–16 year old pupils.

The main theoretical problem – and it did have practical implications – was the fact that there was really no obvious pattern of progression to the history SoAs. Defining progression in historical knowledge, understanding and skills in three (or was it five?) ATs and ten levels was certain to lead to artificiality. The 45 SoAs themselves were criticised on several grounds. Many were unclear and could be interpreted in a variety of ways. Many seemed to be wrongly placed. The level 3 statement in AT3 – pupils should make deductions from historical sources – is actually a good way of assessing able 16 year olds! Level 8 in AT3 – pupils should show how a source which is unreliable can nevertheless be useful – is a concept which many Key Stage 2 pupils can grasp.

AT2, in particular, contained substantial flaws, not least because many teachers did not understand it. It perhaps encouraged teachers to emphasise the provisional nature of historical knowledge although much of the historical record is, in fact, relatively secure. Younger pupils and the less able can be confused by the countless references to the uncertainty of knowing what happened. Besides, understanding of interpretations is dependent on the ideas in AT1 and AT3 and in practice good AT2 work almost invariably became indistinguishable from work towards the other ATs.

There were then, and still are, major concerns about assessment and recording attainment within schools. No one seemed to know precisely what evidence was needed to prove that a child had actually reached a particular level. Given the insecure basis for assessment, it is perhaps not surprising that teachers tended to concentrate on the content in the study units at the expense of the skills in the ATs.

Change

Problems with the National Curriculum as a whole rather than with history in particular led to important changes being made to National Curriculum history.

The Government decided that history was no longer to be compulsory post-14 and that current GCSE syllabi, well-resourced and well-understood, would continue. However, the penalty was that history was effectively relegated from the premier division. The decision also meant that the PoS and ATs worked out on the basis of a 5–16 curriculum now lacked coherence. In the wake of the Dearing review of the whole curriculum, a history team was charged with addressing these issues. Achieving consensus within the committee was obviously not easy and the fact that a minority report was produced and that school history again became a topic for media attention signalled that history, as a school subject, remained a contested concept.

Conclusion

The history we teach in schools is the product of complex, conflicting views about what counts as knowledge and how it should be represented to learners. The subject is no more fixed than any other subject and, just as its nature has been contested, so too will it continue to be contested.

Why does this matter? A principled reason is that teaching claims to be a profession and it is appropriate for professionals to understand the nature of the work they profess.

A pragmatic reason is that research is increasingly showing that teachers who understand the nature and purposes of a school subject see a greater range of possibilities in it and are more likely to work on its central themes. The nature of history is indeed seen differently by different people and at different times. Yet, however it is seen, good quality work depends on teachers having a principled view of the nature of their subject and its purposes. Only then are they in a position to make history into active history, through associating the study of the past with learners' understanding based upon the present. They are then well placed to provide activities and tasks that require learners to be mentally active.

With an understanding of the sorts of things that history has claimed to be, we can turn to a consideration of how history may be learned and taught. From there we proceed, in Chapter 3, to a systematic account of some of the techniques of active history.

CHAPTER 2

Quality, Learning and Teaching History

Towards a general account of learning

Although you will not need to be told that learning is a complicated business, we want to go over some familiar ground so as to help us to be clear about what active history is. We shall argue that active history learning is characteristic of good quality in history education.

In this discussion we shall be treating history as a subject made up of three types of knowledge. There is knowledge of ways of working – of the procedures of historical enquiry, or of skills, as they used to be called. This area of knowledge includes the procedures for handling biased and subjective information and is therefore to do with values issues and judgement. It has sometimes been called 'the evidence approach'. Second, there is the knowledge of concepts, which was stressed by the *Place, Time and Society Project*. It is tempting to call this 'understanding', since concepts have associated with them a host of details that elaborate and clarify the concept. These concepts can take many forms, including substantive concepts such as 'parliament', organising concepts such as 'causation' and, we suggest, understandings of the sort that people of whatever race, culture and time were, however different they might have been from us, people like us in their humanity. Lastly, there is the knowledge of information, so prized by many 'traditionalists', that is to say knowledge of facts, dates and details. This last sort of knowledge is not insignificant, for it has been said that explanation in history consists of going into ever more detail about what happened. Be that as it may, such information is subordinate to the organising function of concepts and to the general methods of enquiry that are history's procedures. Figure 2.1 illustrates this.

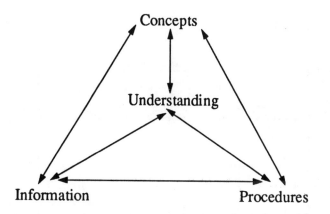

Figure 2.1 Knowledge and understanding

Understanding can take many forms. In the secondary years we may aim for sophisticated understandings, equivalent to high GCSE grades. However, a more modest goal is to foster awarenesses of the past. Awareness may be described as a broad, general grasp of key concepts and procedures, with some information attached to them. We might wish, for example, to engender awareness of fascism and, although a detailed knowledge of Italian, Spanish, English and German forms would be desirable, the prerequisite is a general awareness of the meaning and significance of the term. Equally, an awareness of bias might be no more than a recognition that sources are not always unproblematic, while a more sophisticated understanding would display knowledge of the many ways in which different sources may embody a range of assumptions and other biases.

Having suggested that understanding is a mélange of concepts, information and procedures, let us now turn to the learner and the material to be learned. Figure 2.2 shows some of the possible relationships between the two.

		Dull	The material New history topic	Technically hard	Ambiguous/ contradictory
	Historically aware				▓▓▓
The learner	Intelligent			▓▓▓	
	Motivated		▓▓▓		
	Uninterested	▓▓▓			

Figure 2.2 A variety of learning interactions

The diagonal path across figure 2.2 suggests that the uninterested learner confronted with a dull topic is likely to have a far less promising experience than the intelligent, motivated and historically aware learner who works upon material that is both technically hard and supports different, perhaps contradictory, historical conclusions. Better learning consists of moving encounters towards the top right corner of the grid.

Of course, this over-simplifies things. For one thing, the characteristics listed in figure 2.2 are not objective. What is dull to one person is fascinating to another, and we readily appreciate that difficulty is very much related to each learner's previous achievements and expectations. This is why it is so irritating to be told that we should make work interesting, relevant or suitably easy, as if these were characteristics that can be read off like the temperature on a thermometer, or created at will.

Motivation is a topic that helps us to develop this claim about the subjectivity of learning. Success can enhance learners' motivation, which implies that the way work is monitored and assessed is an important topic. We shall return to it in Chapter 5, simply noting for the moment that the way in which feedback is given can affect motivation, quite independently of other characteristics of the learner and the material. Where feedback emphasises what has been achieved and draws attention, constructively, to a limited number of points for improvement, motivation is better preserved than if the same message is conveyed by stressing the failures and giving no constructive advice for improvement. What seems to be important is what the learner believes to be the source of the learning problems. If the learner attributes them to fixed factors that lie beyond his or her control – to intelligence, for example – it is not surprising if the conclusion is that nothing can be done and that it makes sense to give up. If, on the other hand, achievement is attributed to factors which do lie within the learner's power – to the amount of effort, for example – it is possible to sustain motivation in the face of some failure.

Returning to figure 2.2, we are hoping for a student who is not only motivated but also disposed to attribute any setbacks to factors within her or his command. This is why it is important for teachers to stress the positive in learners' work and to make clear what can be done to bring about further achievement.

Two further dimensions complicate the learning pattern sketched in figure 2.2. One is the environment in which learning takes place and its attendant expectations, and the other is the tasks that shape the learning activity.

The resources available for learning have an obvious effect, although research has consistently failed to find a direct link between learning achievement and environmental variables such as class size, expenditure per pupil and the provision of any form of resources. Other environmental factors that can affect learning are the expectations that learners and other significant people hold about the place, value and likely success of learning, and the nature of the school. In recent years a lot of work has been done that has indicated that students' 'life chances' are significantly affected by the schools they attend. Schools do, it seems, make a difference to the quality of learning, although there are some indications (Smith and Tomlinson, 1991) that subject departments may have a powerful effect as well. Whatever line one takes on these arguments, quality learning is not simply the product of what happens in the classroom, for that is itself shaped by a variety of environmental factors.

Tasks tell us how to react to material. Material that may be quite understandable at one level, even quite enjoyable, may become something quite different given a task structure that makes unpleasant demands upon us. Tasks determine what we do and what we provide as evidence of achievement. Tasks carry with them criteria of success and failure and become the currency in which our academic worth is measured. What the learner brings to the class, the nature of the material before the learner, and other factors that impinge upon the learning, all come second to the demands of the task. We can say, then, that quality learning takes place when tasks are appropriate and is obstructed where they are not. We shall shortly return to the question of what makes for effective tasks.

We have outlined a view of learning as the interaction of *learner* and *material* under the influence of *tasks* within an *environment*. Each of these four factors has its own dimensions of complexity, complexities that often can neither be described nor predicted objectively but can only be appreciated and understood subjectively. Good quality history work takes place when the teacher has sufficient knowledge and artistry to set tasks, within a given environment, that encourage interactions between learners and historical material of the sort shown in the top right hand area of figure 2.2. In order to develop this, we need to add an account of how learning takes place.

When new information comes before us, there are three broad responses:

1. Ignore it – as we do with so much that is on the news, in the papers and all around us. At best, most of the information we encounter flits across our consciousness and is gone; much more we simply never notice.

2. Assimilate it. This is when we take in new information and file it away in existing slots. Thus, I read that there was no 'last stand' at the Little Big Horn in 1876, which sufficiently catches my imagination for it to be remembered and assimilated into my ideas about that battle. What I read doesn't particularly surprise me and I have no need to rearrange my thoughts about Custer.

3. Accommodate our thinking to fit it. This is quite rare, coming about when new information doesn't fit existing ideas and cannot be ignored or written off as insignificant. Thus, a 1648 pamphlet about the uprising in Canterbury got ignored because I was unwilling to change my ideas about the English Civil War, but Warren's book on King John led me to accommodate my existing ideas to take account of his thesis.

Much learning takes the form of assimilation. Accommodation needs to happen as well so that our ideas about people, the past, power relations, causation, change, progress, and values in human affairs are changed by our history learning. The American psychologist Norman (1978) suggests that complex learning has a four-phase structure. Initially, he says, we accumulate information, which is akin to assimilation. Then, often as the result of skilful teaching, we may restructure our thinking, achieving a new understanding, rather like accommodation. This new understanding should then be applied to problems and other tasks in order to consolidate it, before giving way to copious practice in order to automate it.

Although the theory was developed to explain how whole subjects are mastered, it seems to us to apply also to the way new ideas and procedures might be learned in history. Take, for example, the notion that historical knowledge is based upon interpretation of sources, as set out in Table 2.1.

Stage in the learning cycle	Learner's understanding of the place of primary sources in history
Stage 1 – Accumulation of knowledge (assimilation)	Learner becomes aware that history doesn't just come from books but is based, to some degree, on understanding primary sources.
Stage 2 – Restructuring (accommodation)	Learner understands that history is an interpretation of the past based on surviving sources.
Stage 3 – Application	Learner works on tasks that depend upon this new insight – tasks that might encourage the learner to revert to the idea that history comes from books *and* to see that this is inadequate.
Stage 4 – Tuning	Over time the learner faces plenty of tasks that assume the routine application of the new insight, so that it becomes ingrained and applied automatically.

Table 2.1 A learning cycle and history learning

If this model is acceptable, three things follow from it:

1. We need to be quite clear about the key concepts, insights and procedures that we are trying to develop.

2. We need to think about their development across the whole of the secondary phase, since while we might tackle stages 1 and 2 in a term, some learners will need to re-visit these stages later because the ideas failed to take, while all learners will need to apply and tune the concepts and procedures over the following years. It's worth stressing that Norman expected stage 4 to involve 'massive practice' – something that is rather unfashionable in certain quarters.

3. Different types of tasks will be more appropriate to different stages in the learning cycle. The next chapter is organised around this idea and develops it. Here we will just say that we are not setting up a rigid classification of tasks, since essays, to take a familiar type of task, can work for any of the four stages. The same is true of some other tasks as well. However, we shall suggest that certain types of task have greatest power when used at certain points of the learning cycle.

We are claiming, then, that history should be active history to the degree that it entails the mental activity of restructuring our understandings. We have not claimed, nor shall we claim, that active history means that learners should run around and physically do things.

We are saying that if active history is taken to mean just physically active history it has become trivialised, and we can see no reason to expect that the resultant learning will be especially effective. Take a field trip, for example. This is certainly a physical activity, as learners see, sketch, walk, measure, sit, record, photograph, shop and go. Yet it is entirely possible that little learning takes place, or that nothing beyond stage 1 happens. If learners are to make sense of the fieldwork, to identify the key points of it and to reach new understandings, they need to be more than observers. They need to be engaged in thinking about the site – about the meaning of the remains, about uses and anomalies, about people, purposes and problems. Without tasks to prompt this mental activity, a site visit might amount to nothing more than tourist memories of who was sick in the bus and the hot dog stand in the grounds.

It is useful to draw on a distinction made by researchers into Higher Education. Some students, they claim, have a 'surface' approach to learning, aiming to memorise and reproduce the content that they encounter. Others have a 'deep' approach, which involves trying to rework the material, to make sense of it in terms of their own learning and to develop their own understanding. It can be said that understanding does not go with a 'surface' approach but depends upon a 'deep' approach. In order to promote 'deep' approaches, tutors are advised to set work that cannot be done successfully by a simple learn and tell strategy. Essentially, they are advised to set work that requires active learning, using methods of the sort that we are recommending. This is consistent with psychological research demonstrating that more information is remembered, and better remembered, if learners have had to be active – that is, to think and work on problematic aspects. Memorisation is improved through active learning. The bonus is that better understanding goes with it.

But how does active learning fit with stages 3 and 4 of our learning cycle, with their concern for application and tuning? We approach this through the oblique question of whether we learn when we're not conscious of learning. Common sense says that we do, and some people would say that much human learning takes this form. But what happens to this 'incidental' learning? Where is it 'filed' in the brain? How easy is it to retrieve learning that happened below our threshold of awareness? It appears that we may locate this learning by accident but it's obviously quite hard to make purposeful use of learning that we are hardly conscious of having. This leads us to two propositions:

1. It is easiest to make use of learning if we are aware of what it is that we have learned, understood and are able to do.

2. Teaching should encourage learners to be aware of what it is they

know, understand and can do, and help them to learn when and how to apply this learning.

We shall soon look at teaching in more detail but here we want to keep with learning. If good learning involves a consciousness about what has been learned, what is sometimes called 'metacognition', then the application and tuning of this learning will also be conscious, or active. What we are saying is that learners ought to be encouraged to think about the insights and procedures that are best applied to problems (stage 3) and that it is only when they become expert at this (stage 4) that we might find it hard to talk of active learning, simply because the learners' thinking may, in this respect, have become automated.

Thus, active history means providing tasks that encourage restructuring and metacognition – the thoughtful application of prior learning. Active history also implies the use of a variety of tasks, partly because different tasks are more or less powerful for different learning purposes, but also because learning depends upon motivation. We have said that an important factor in motivation is helping learners to attribute their performance to things within their control, such as effort and thoughtfulness. It also depends on interest, and although we have said that it is unpredictable to a degree, there is wide agreement that variety helps to enhance interest. If we wish learners to be well-disposed to active history, then a breadth of tasks is needed.

Learning history

There might be some unease at our use of general learning theory to address history learning. After all, is not history a unique subject? As we have said, the Schools' History Project has substantially shaped our thinking about school history. Distinctive is 'its insistence on going beyond methodology and stressing human agency, causal explanation, developmental narrative and evidence-based methodology' (Shemilt, undated, p.1). Lee (1983, p.48) said that 'the particular logical features which distinguish history from other forms of knowledge...are its narrative structure, colligatory organization, its concern with human action and rational explanation'. Not only does this imply that there might be special difficulties in history learning, but it has also been claimed that consequently we need a separate account of learning, understanding and achievement in school history. History learning involves working with subtle procedures, developing and applying abstract concepts (such as causation, communism, revolution and time), and working with complex information, usually to do with the politics of dead white European males. Given children's limited understanding of the modern world of grown ups, history can be painted as a pretty fierce subject. The prominence of reading and writing in school history compounds the problem for many learners.

Despite this 'psycho-gloom', history teachers know that despite the problems, it *is* possible to promote lively awarenesses of the past with children – even with Infants. Further research confirmed that substantial achievements *are* possible in primary and secondary phases (e.g. Booth, 1979; Shemilt, 1980; West, 1981; Ashby and Lee, 1987; Knight, 1987a; Cooper, 1992). However, several of these researchers argued that their research showed that historical reasoning is distinctive and cannot be contained within general learning theories. History, it was said, is creative, not deductive, about making connections, seeking insights, telling stories and drawing on existing insights into people and the world.

This fits well with developments in psychology which emphasise that learning proceeds at different rates in different areas, or domains. Skill in a domain is increasingly being seen as the result of extensive practice and of plenty of knowledge. We speak of domain-specific learning and of domain-specific expertise, with the implication that what we know, understand and can do in a domain is not unrelated to our general ability but is also affected by the quality and quantity of our engagement with it.

But there are suggestions that our ability to work in a domain is not disconnected from our more general abilities. Knight (1987a) shows that children's reasoning about people in the past is similar to their reasoning about people in the present, and work by Smith and Knight (1992) suggests that their reasoning with history material is barely different from their logical thinking in general. Research which led to claims that history learning is distinctive enough to need its own theory may simply have been misconceived.

This view leads to the position that there are, indeed, things about history learning that teachers need to take very seriously but that there is no reason why ideas about good learning, such as we have already sketched out, cannot be applied to history, albeit with attention to history's special needs.

This connection between learners' general thinking and their understanding of history can be seen when we examine the place of 'empathy' in school history. Learners apply their knowledge about people in the present to account for the actions of people in the past and use similar scripts to explain the actions of people in the past and life in the present. Some of these are recognisably comic book scripts, while others are naive. It has been said that adolescents often hold a 'doppo' theory of history, assuming that people in the past were rather dense, much as portrayed by Terry Pratchett:

> The class was learning about some revolt in which some peasants had wanted to stop being peasants and, since the nobles had won, had stopped being peas-

ants *really quickly*. Had they bothered to learn to read and acquire some history books, they'd have learned about the uncertain merits of things like scythes and pitchforks when used in a battle against crossbows and broadswords. (*Soul Music*, published by Victor Gollancz, 1994, p.34).

A commoner adolescent view is that people in the past – and people in the present – are morally inferior to the learner (Knight, 1987a). Carretero and colleagues (1994) have made the related observation that adolescents tend to try and explain events in the past mainly in terms of people's actions, whereas skilled historians set these actions in the context of more abstract forces, such as economic and social change. Both draw on the concept of human agency but adolescents are not good at taking account of the setting within which people acted – they tend to trivialise when they explain other people's lives, whether in the present or the past.

What we see is a connection between history learning and other learning. History depends upon learners understanding how complicated human action is and it has, in turn, the power to help learners to move away from seeing the human world in stereotypical and simple forms.

While we do not want to deny that there are special things to keep in mind in history teaching, as there are in maths, RE and science teaching, we reject the position that says that history is so distinctive a subject that we need a separate theory of learning and development to account for it. A major problem is that learners apply their imperfect thinking about the present to produce imperfect reasoning about the past. As we move to look at the teaching of history, we shall look at how some of these special concerns might be handled, always in the spirit that what we say about history teaching and learning will generally hold good, to some degree, for other subjects too.

Teaching for active learning

It is easy to identify rank bad teaching, but describing and recognising quality teaching is far harder and far more open to argument than most inspection and appraisal schemes recognise. We can reject the idea that effective teachers share certain personal characteristics, for research has found no evidence that this is so. Indeed, international studies of teaching effectiveness yield no firm conclusions about what makes for effective teaching (Anderson and Burns, 1989), although there is no shortage of suggestions about good teaching (see Knight, 1993, for a fuller discussion of this).

In theory, the best way of identifying quality teaching is to say that it leads to greater-than-expected gains in learning. To identify it, we would need to assess, reliably and validly, learners' mastery of history at the beginning of a course and again at the end of the course, using the same measurement scale. The difference between the two measures would show learners' progress in history, from which we could infer that good (or indifferent) teaching had taken place. The recent experience of National Curriculum testing in England shows that this approach is full of technical problems and that it is of no help at present.

Recognising that any account of effective history teaching will not be based on compelling research evidence, and insisting that there are many ways of promoting quality learning in the history classroom, we nevertheless offer 12 pointers to effective history teaching, keeping in mind our own experience and the literature on teaching and learning, both generally and in history.

1. Departmental management

We must begin with the assumption that teachers have authority in their classrooms. Given teachers who are in authority, what can be done to prevent active history from compromising classroom stability?

Clearly, learners' expectations are a major problem. This has two sides to it. The first is that if a department consistently promotes these ways of working learners will be socialised into seeing them as normal. When this starts with the more pliant learners of Year 7, routines for active history learning can become ingrained. The big problem arises when there is no deliberate, departmental-wide socialisation of this sort. It is not surprising, then, if Year 9 learners react badly to the introduction of threatening learning methods, and if it seems to take an age to get them to understand what to do, and how.

Active history is a whole department matter.

2. Classroom management

There is plenty of research which shows that teachers may be employed to help learners to understand many, often abstract things, but in the classroom the emphasis has to be on routines and order. Teaching more than about 15 learners pushes classroom management issues to the fore. We do not mean that large numbers of learners are necessarily harder to control than small groups, but rather that greater numbers of learners make more calls on teachers' attention by way of requests for help, problems with lost work or equipment, and the need to give feedback about their work to individuals. Necessarily, teachers cope with these pressures by trying to reduce the incidence of these calls for attention: by setting routine work, by whole class teaching, by simple assessment systems, by setting no, little or undemanding homework. Their performance is still virtuoso, with studies of primary phase teachers showing that they have between 150 and 200 interchanges with children per hour. Yet, busy though they are, the price is that active history can be crowded out of the repertoire. After all, active history, which should pose problems and make children think, *will* lead to more calls for help.

Learners collude in this 'routinisation' of classroom work. Doyle (1983) referred to this as a grade-performance exchange. Learners normally wish to get good grades, or at least to avoid bad grades. To do that they need to know what routines to use in order to succeed. If they are given work that does not yield to routine practices they call for help and try to 'bargain the task down' by getting the teacher to give cues and advice to make it simpler. Where they know what to do, learners will normally get on with their work, allowing the classroom to function smoothly. So, comprehension activities can be very acceptable to learners, whereas work on problematic sources can lead to many learners going 'off task', causing disruption to the classroom routine.

In this sense, active history is harder than normal history because it makes learners think – which can be uncomfortable. Teaching actively means not just being skilled in routine classroom management, but also having 'withitness', being able to 'dangle', manage transitions smoothly, scan, be clear, etc., in the complex setting of active history. Skilled primary teachers do it all of the time.

3. Teachers' manner

Research into learners' ideas about what makes for good teachers says that they value teachers who explain things well, who have time for the learners, who are not sarcastic or overbearing but who do keep order in the classroom, and who have a sense of humour.

4. Subject understanding

It seems obvious that history teachers should know some history. Some, who teach history as their second or third subject, may not know very much, and from time to time HMI expressed concern about the mismatch between what teachers taught and their subject specialism. However, knowing some history is not enough. Shemilt's Schools Council 13–16 History Project evaluation (1980), found that learners did best when taught by teachers who best understood the Project philosophy. More recently, Wilson and Wineberg (1988) have shown how different beliefs about the nature and purpose of school history lead to very different ways of teaching it. The teacher who sees the job as conveying information is unlikely to teach history well, since, as we have argued, history learning involves learning concepts and procedures too. These are not to be gained from simply acquiring information.

Following from the previous chapter, we claim that quality history teaching depends on teachers knowing some history but, far more importantly, they need to understand what history is, to grasp its distinctive structure and to seek to help learners towards an awareness of it. The teacher who has such knowledge is in a position to teach a new topic effectively, whereas the teacher who lacks it may master the same information but face problems in trying to clarify what it is *for*, and see no need to apply it to the development of skill in historical procedures, to concept development and to metacognitive awareness. Unsurprisingly, the teacher who does not understand the structures of history is hardly able to make it more than a pile of facts, a series of quaint stories and an apparent irrelevance in the curriculum.

5. Clarity of purpose

Effective teachers are clear about goals. They know what are the key basic ideas or procedures that they want to develop with *this* material and with *these* learners, and they don't let this get overlaid by the clutter of information.

Better still, they share this clarity with learners, explaining what the significance or purpose of this piece of work is. Bearing in mind that we are speaking about key awarenesses, we suggest that effective history teachers say what they are going to say, say it, and then say they've said it.

6. Key concepts

Part of this clarity lies in having a firm grasp of the key concepts to be worked through in history. It is possible to identify a long hierarchy of concepts but here we will focus on just two sorts – the large, organising concepts of history (time, evidence, causation, change, effects and continuity) and the broad substantive concepts such as 'revolution', 'medieval', 'government' and 'economic'. In most cases the problem is not so much that learners lack the concept but that they have an alternative meaning for it, so that a cause is something that comes before something else, evidence is information, and parliament is a corrupt racket. As in science, the teacher's job is to identify these faulty concepts and then to help learners move towards better ones.

Shemilt (1980, 1984) did much to identify the sequence of concepts that are typically held by adolescents and reference to these enables teachers to see what faulty ideas learners are likely to have, as well to identify better ideas that might replace the faulty ideas until even better ones can take their place. The old National Curriculum for history (DES, 1990) contains much of this thinking in the level statements for the attainment targets relating to these organising concepts and it is still well worth using when planning for concept development. It hardly needs to be said that developing these concepts will be a perennial concern throughout the secondary years and a history department needs to have a view, as a department, of how the sequence of development is likely to work out across the five years of secondary schooling.

One of history's great problems is that there are so many concepts – or terms – that have meanings that differ from learners' daily, uncomplicated usage that it is impossible to identify, let alone to cover, all of them. This is no reason for not being alert to the more important of them, and substantive concepts such as 'society', 'church', 'colonisation' and 'democracy' should also be thought about on a five-year scale.

7. Metacognition

Effective teachers help learners to be aware of the key ideas and procedures and make opportunities for these ideas and procedures to be purposefully used. Metacognition, then, is thinking about thinking, or knowing what you know. Learners are encouraged to think metacognitively through planning their work, through discussing their plans with one another and through some forms of self- and peer-assessment.

8. Depth

Understanding concepts, mastering procedures, thinking metacognitively, being an active learner and grasping something of the structure of history all depend on working in depth. We insist, though, that depth is only valuable if the depth of information is used to develop the organising principles and procedures of history on the lines of the learning cycle that we have described. If depth amounts to detailed information and no more, it is as otiose as superficial breadth.

But does this not still fall foul of the National Curriculum requirements for the core study units? We suggest not, while recognising that they could be read that way. The requirements say which topics must be covered: they do not say in how much detail, or imply that all aspects must be covered even-handedly. Case studies and local history can carry many aspects of a topic and what is left may be read in as a piece of bridging narrative, used to set the scene for the next case study.

9. Teaching strategically

Some years ago the hottest dispute in primary education was whether the 'traditional' or the 'progressive' teaching style was the best. The sterility of the argument was exposed when it was seen that effective teaching was possible within either style and that, in any case, most teachers used a blend of 'styles'. Strategic teaching, drawing on a range of methods for a range of purposes for different learners, offers the best hope of teaching in a way that is fit for the purpose. Adherence to one method or routine may be an important coping strategy but it is limited. For example, there are people who swear by group work. Certainly, it has advantages but research (Peterson, 1979) suggests that it is best suited to tasks where opinions and judgements are wanted and where the evidence to substantiate them needs to be tested. There is also a lot of evidence that group work can be ineffective (Galton and Williamson, 1992) and we draw the conclusion that it, like any other teaching method, ought to be used strategically. And let us be quite clear that we say the same about exposition, which also has an enduring and important place in humanities learning (Cuban, 1991).

10. Assessment of learning

We shall develop this theme in Chapter 6. Here we notice that it is the tasks we set learners that shape their learning. Those tasks are typically assessed by the teacher, implying that assessment, in this sense, is a powerful force in ordering classroom learning. It is most potent when the tasks are well conceived (and not just a set of comprehension questions) and when useful feedback on performance is quickly given to learners. This may be through comments in the classroom (preferably positive comments – teachers usually criticise far more than they praise), or through marking work. In all cases, it is important to encourage learners to attribute performance to factors within their control and to identify key points for development that relate to the main ideas or procedures that are being promoted. Detailed feedback may not be very helpful.

11. Going beyond the text

Published textbooks are the staple of the history classroom. However good the text, it is not by any means sufficient for quality learning. Not only are there difficulties embedded in the medium (Hull, 1985), but they cannot be sensitive to the way that *this* department is trying to foster awareness of core concepts and procedures. Textbook publishers, like schools broadcasters, insist that their books are resources to be used. In pressured classrooms they can be the curriculum rather than resources to support it.

Good history teaching *uses* texts. And ideally, it uses books from more than one series, allowing learners to see how the same topic is handled differently by different writers, thus showing the extent to which history is an interpretation of sources.

12. Differentiation

A recurrent difficulty is organising classrooms so that learners with different levels of achievement and different perspectives find work that is matched to them. This is, of course, an ideal situation but that does not mean that it is not a worthwhile goal to aim for. All classes are mixed ability classes to a greater or lesser degree. We identify four broad strategies for responding to this range:

1. Set open-ended tasks that learners can tackle at their own level of understanding. The classic essay or project represents this approach. While it can tell teachers a lot about what learners know, understand and can do, this method offers learners little help in doing better.

2. Set focused tasks, probably based on the old National Curriculum statements of attainment, which address specific ideas or procedures. These tasks might be used for diagnostic purposes, so that learners working at level 5, or showing a certain misconception, go on to work designed to move them ahead.

3. Set stepped tasks, in which the initial questions may be tapping a level 5 understanding on the old National Curriculum, with later questions moving through to higher levels.

4. Use mixed ability groups, drawing on the insight that both the more able and the less able can benefit from working in such a group where the task demands that they work together (Perret-Clermont, 1980).

However, we need to be sensitive to more than just ability differences. We have already mentioned the range of differences in learning style and motivation. We also need to think about differences in race and gender, both in terms of how we teach and what we teach.

Take gender and classroom organisation. It is well known that vocal boys will dominate classrooms and take the lion's share of the teacher's attention. Moreover, keeping the classroom running smoothly leads teachers to collude with this imbalance. A minimal conclusion is that, when thinking about active history, teachers ought to consider whether certain activities are likely to lead to male dominance and, if so, whether learners might benefit from working in same sex groups.

Or take race and the content of the history curriculum. Most modern textbooks have sloughed off the racialist stereotypes of earlier generations but there is still reason to ask how people of different races are portrayed in the story of the progress of the British nation from the Romans to VE Day. Much the same can be said about the treatment of women in history books, which is better than it was but which still usually fails to ask systematically about women's lives.

Differences of race and gender are likely to mean that learners bring to the classroom perspectives which teachers might not call to mind in their daily work. Women, for example, are often said to be more interested in people and their emotional lives than in technical and abstract matters and, given that both perspectives are valid, it is worth asking how the curriculum caters for such differences in interest. Similarly, people's cultural backgrounds, whether shaped by class or by race and religion, exert a profound influence on the range of concepts, understandings and assumptions that they bring to their school history. Failure to appreciate this can lead to history that deals in misconceptions – teachers taking it for granted that children see the world in a white middle class way. We are not taking the strong line that these differences are such that there is no common ground, but we are saying that they are significant enough for us to think twice when teaching history. In what sense can we use the word 'God' in a multi-faith class?

Differences of ability are just the most obvious of the differences that learners bring to the supremely social subject of history and which affect their engagement with it. Good teaching can never get this complexity right but it can recognise and begin to react to it through differentiation.

Summary

We have outlined a case for valuing active learning and proceeded to discuss some of the factors that are associated with effective teaching for active learning in history. We now turn to some of the techniques that can be used to promote active learning through active teaching.

CHAPTER 3

Teaching Active History – Classroom Activities and Tasks

Introduction

In this chapter we shall describe a range of active history methods in the knowledge that every one of them can be modified in many ways and that there are methods we have not included, often because they are quite complicated to describe. We have said relatively little about 'evidence-based' tasks, mainly because these are common – arguably too common. In the next chapter we shall draw upon this set of methods as we outline some active ways of tackling KS3 and KS4 units.

First, a recap of the principles underpinning active history work:

- We are primarily interested in mental activity.
- Active history tasks need to be purposeful.
- We expect active history work to be varied and hence motivating.
- The tasks that we set are the key to active history.
- Depth studies are preferred.
- School texts vary in the degree to which they promote active history but even the best are no more than resources for it.

It should go without saying that tasks will be designed so that non-history activities are kept to a necessary minimum. What we have in mind is cutting down the amount of time that is spent on mechanical English (copying out long sections of notes), on drawing map, graph and table outlines, copying diagrams and illustrations, colouring in and designing project title pages. This is not to deny that history can, as we shall argue in Chapter 6, contribute much to other parts of the curriculum and ought to be seen to do so.

Take colouring in as an example of an activity that is often a 'busywork' task but which can help history learning. One of us has a task in which learners are given a 17th century English description of a native Virginian and asked to sketch a picture of this Amerindian. This is a translation exercise, requiring learners to engage closely with the source as they translate it from one medium to another. The purpose is to break learners away from the view that native Americans conformed to the stereotype of the Plains Indians ('Heap bad men. Scalp 'em quick'). Not only does it do this effectively, but it also forces learners to read the source carefully, since errors – like not seeing that these people were brown, not red – are quickly noticed as the drawing emerges. Putting a time limit on this task, as we try to do with most tasks, helps to restrain any tendencies to make a high artistic production out of it, keeping the historical purposes to the fore. Learners' pictures are then displayed, along with the 17th century pictures that John White drew of the natives of a neighbouring tribe. Why, learners are asked, are there differences between the pictures? What are the implications of these differences? Art, we see, is used as a servant of history, not as a substitute.

Organising principles

We have arranged the methods that we describe under three headings. Some tasks are especially well suited to acquiring information, which broadly represents the first stage of the learning cycle that we describe in the previous chapter, accumulation of knowledge. The second grouping, based upon stage two, is called 'working on information'. Our third grouping, which we call 'pulling together', combines the stages of 'application' and 'tuning'. We decided not to retain the distinction made in the original model (Table 2.1) on the grounds that, while it is psychologically useful, we could not distinguish between types of classroom activities intended to promote restructuring and those intended to tune new understandings and skills. Certainly, as the literature on science education shows, tasks can be set for these different purposes, but we did not see that the types of task employed would necessarily differ between the two purposes.

We are conscious that activities can be used for a variety of purposes, so that when we identify 'diamond factor ranking' as an activity well suited to working on information we are aware that it can also be used for pulling together new skills and insights. This holds true for most of the activities we describe. However, if this is kept in mind, we still believe that the way we have organised these activities is useful for teachers who are planning work with a view of learning in mind.

In our discussion of these activities we are assuming that wherever possible teachers have printed sheets for learners to work on. It is hardly active history if good tasks have first to be copied out, maps traced and charts reproduced. Nor does it necessarily follow that learners will retain the information they copy.

Activities that enable learners to acquire information

The central problem for history (indeed all) teachers is to persuade children to make an active effort to learn. Making history interesting is the key to success, a fact recognised by those who drew up the GCSE National Criteria and by the 1990 HWG. Interest can be aroused by the subject matter and/or through teaching methods.

The content of history

Over the last two decades the historical intelligentsia has been more concerned with what children should know in history rather than with what children might want to know. The only educational theorist who has seriously explored the question of what content children like (and why) is Kieran Egan. He propounds the notion that there are four stages of educational development: mythic, romantic, philosophic and ironic. He claims that most children from the age of c.9–16 are at the 'romantic' stage of development (for example, Egan 1979). They need/want to develop a sense of the limits of the real world and tend to enjoy the kind of content which fills *The Guinness Book of Records* and *The News of the World*: it is the strange and bizarre that engages and is most accessible, not the near at hand and local.

Egan's views have been largely ignored by history educationists, despite the fact that he draws many of his examples from history. It is easy to see why. At bottom he provides us with little more than a simplistic stage theory and offers little evidence that children are as he depicts them. His stages are far from clear-cut and his thumb-nail sketches of how his ideas might work out in practice are far from convincing.

Nevertheless, some of his ideas strike a responsive chord. He provides an explanation for the popularity of 'blood and guts' history: a rarely discussed phenomenon (perhaps because it is seen as trivialising the subject) but one which is well-exploited by most history teachers. Egan is right to point out the false assumption that history which is in evidence in the pupils' immediate environment is interesting whereas medieval history, for example, is uninteresting. In Egan's view the 'bizarre' societies and people of medieval England are more accessible to most pupils than much local history. Egan is right to emphasise the need for dramatic detail. He is right to claim that many researchers have ignored children's ability to imagine and fantasise. He is also right to stress the importance of content, and he recognises that children need much more knowledge about the world and human experience than they sometimes receive. An obsession with skills and cognitive development has for too long blinded some to the fact that for the learner the personal significance of history is often bound up with its content, and arises from consideration of value issues and the making of judgements.

'Romantic' content does not guarantee success. Different topics go down well (or badly) with different groups and individuals and much depends on the individual teacher. A teacher's enthusiasm can often 'sell' a topic. Arguably any topic can be made interesting if presented well, but we suspect that some – often bizarre and gory – topics are popular regardless of who is teaching them and how they are being taught. Henry VIII's six wives interest pupils far more than the Reformation; Rasputin goes down better than the Russian Revolution.

Given that there are no absolute criteria for deciding what is important and non-trivial in history, pupils' interests should be an important criterion for content selection. Pupils are likely to work more effectively if they are given content they enjoy.

That said, we turn to some of the commonly used methods of enabling pupils to acquire historical information.

Teacher (and other) talk

History teachers frequently introduce a new topic by talking about it. This style has often been slammed by those who advocate active learning. We advocate active learning but not to the exclusion of teacher talk. Talk is essential: it can be a vital way of sparking pupils' interest.

Storytelling

Storytelling is one of the most basic and important weapons in a history teacher's armoury. A. J. P. Taylor claimed that, 'we shouldn't be ashamed to admit that history at bottom is simply a form of storytelling...there is no escaping the fact that the original task of the historian is to answer the question: "What happened next"' (1983, pp. 113–4). Good storytelling is one of most potent ways of explaining to children the events of the past and transferring the teacher's enthusiasm to the class as a whole. It is especially important with children whose literacy skills are deficient, but many able children also find that the printed page lacks the sparkle and excitement of a spoken story.

We much prefer storytelling to storyreading. This is not to say that there is not a place for reading: there are excellent texts which are well worth reading to a class. But there are enormous differences between telling and reading. A storyteller can interact with a class in a way that is hard when chained to a book, the text of which can wipe out all natural speech rhythms, mannerisms and eye contact.

A good storytelling session depends on a harmony of three things – the story, the qualities of the storyteller, and the nature of the audience.

A good story needs a strong, straightforward plot, a few main characters with whom pupils can readily identify, plenty of action, drama and suspense, a colourful background, detail and humour. The events of 1066 make an excellent story, as do executions and deaths which can sustain the flagging interest of a class and ensure that pupils pay some attention to more important, but less intrinsically interesting, matters to follow.

Effective storytellers come in all shapes and forms. Some are highly dramatic: others soft-voiced and reserved. Either style, and a range in between, can be effective. Some teachers are 'born' storytellers but most learn the hard way, developing with practice. A good memory and faith in the story are essential: if the story appeals to you then it stands a better chance of appealing to the audience.

The best storyteller, armed with the best story, has to take into account the age, sophistication and interests of the class. Storytelling involves constant interaction between the teller and the audience. There is a need to adjust pace, tone and texture according to the class's response. Nor should the story be a monologue. There are invariably opportunities to ask questions and thus involve the pupils in some form of dialogue.

Radio

Schools radio broadcasts, which are clearly related to storytelling, remain an under-used resource. It is difficult to know why this is. Programme-makers can call upon skilled actors and can usually reconstruct the past and tell a story much better than an individual teacher. Yet teachers seem reluctant to use radio broadcasts: perhaps they are unaware of what is on offer or believe that radio programmes simply do not excite children sufficiently.

Guest speakers

Another approach is to bring in guest speakers. Reminiscences of elderly people can add colour and depth to history and a new dimension to pupils' understanding. However, there are dangers. Some speakers have no rapport with the pupils and ramble on to everyone's embarrassment.

Explanation, question and answer

Teacher explanation is an essential part of the teaching-learning process. Involving pupils in the explanation process is also essential. Questions, which can help pupils clarify their ideas and extend their understanding, are the main way of doing this. It is a common claim that many questions which teachers ask orally are closed questions, tapping a narrow range of mental abilities and requiring little more than monosyllabic responses. The remedies are ostensibly simple but practically complex. The received wisdom is to ask more open and divergent questions, encouraging pupils to make additional comments, interpretations and judgements. But unfortunately experience suggests this rarely works. Many pupils simply fail to respond! Good questioning involves a mixture of closed and open questions and the focus needs to be on the chains of questions that are asked, not upon individual questions. The chains should be worthwhile and constructed in a way which children can follow.

Textbooks and worksheets

Given that much of the raw material of history is written evidence, reading skills play a critical role in children's ability to 'do' history. 'Books', declared the HWG (DES, 1990, p.177) 'remain the most important single resource for learning history'. We would not disagree too much with this – although we regard the teacher as the most important single resource.

There are some excellent books on the market which provide good text, imaginative sources, lavish illustrations and a range of tasks. Unfortunately, relatively few are simple linguistically and conceptually and at the same time 'mature' and interesting, which makes the plight of youngsters with poor literacy skills even worse. On top of this, many teachers assume that pupils have acquired the basic reading skills at primary school and that reading requires little further attention after 11. Many pupils, in fact, do need support and it is unsatisfactory simply to ask them to read a certain number of pages, offering them nothing by way of guidance or follow-up.

It is obviously important that teachers select appropriate textbooks for pupils. There are a number of readability formulae, encompassing a wide variety of features. Vocabulary and sentence length are the best overall indicators of difficulty but readability scores should not exempt the teacher from making decisions about the appropriateness of the written material. However, do bear in mind that readability formulae give the reading age needed to cope *independently* with a text. Harder texts can be managed by groups or in supported classroom activities.

Thankfully, few history teachers are satisfied with a single textbook, however good. Most cull ideas from a number of books and then often produce their own worksheets. Word-processing and photocopying have enabled schools to produce good quality material so that publishers' main advantage is colour. However, there is the danger that many pupils endure daily the pain of 'death by a thousand worksheets'. This is not to deny the need for worksheets. They are essential, but they need to be produced and used with care. The best worksheets, in our view, use simple language, are attractively presented, and pose a historical problem which the pupils have to solve. McIver (1982) has some good ideas for producing worksheets for pupils with special educational needs.

Children must work with varied forms of written primary and secondary sources but these often need adapting to turn them into resources which pupils enjoy handling. Teachers are also vital in terms of explaining the context of the sources, although sometimes pupils can be given carefully chosen material and left to make what they can of it.

The visual dimension

One way of ensuring that reading difficulties do not always get in the way of historical thinking is for teachers to emphasise the visual dimension. 'The visual image', wrote Unwin (1981, p.5) 'has largely replaced the written word as our principal means of communication'. Research by Rogers (1984) indicated that pupils of all abilities preferred working with visual material, which also helped their understanding.

The 'still' image

Improvements in photocopying have ensured that teachers can get mass copies of a variety of visual primary material – paintings, portraits, adverts, posters, cartoons, photographs, and maps. In our view secondary sources – artists' impressions – are equally important, although some text-books seem to go out of their way to eschew them. Good drawings/paintings can capture the imagination, while simple line drawings, especially illustrated diagrams, often provide tremendous information. Cartoons can also be highly effective in helping pupils to understand difficult concepts.

The 'still' image, in all its many forms, can be used simply as an aid to learning. But sometimes examination of a visual source or sources can be the main focus of a lesson. Unwin (1981) has a variety of ideas for using the visual image, including making deductions, describing what is going on, spotting differences, drawing inferences, determining the bias of the image producer, etc. This can be supported through the use of the overlay keyboard, which can make learning to read pictures an enjoyable and his-torically valuable activity.

Film

Teachers are in danger of being swamped by the wealth of film – feature films, general output programmes and school educational programmes – that the video has made available. There is no doubt that film can provide a common educational experience which motivates, regardless of levels of ability. Film can make distant archaeological sites, buildings and artefacts accessible, and help to bring remote events and people to life.

Fortunately, a great deal of the 20th century has been captured on film. Pupils can see Hitler at Nuremburg, witness the D-day landings, experience fighting in Vietnam. It is a sobering thought that up to the 1890s no one left behind any direct visual record of a change of facial expression or a bodily movement. An appreciation of that fact should make us more aware of the importance of film as a primary source which conveys a vast amount of information with great economy. Potentially film, whether primary 'actuality' or secondary reconstruction, can offer an experience of the past and sustain attention in a way that cannot be matched by other means.

We accept that film is not an educational panacea. It has not the attraction it once had for pupils: there is a danger of over-exposure. But we do believe that most of the criticisms of film as a teaching aid are easily answered. The charge that film encourages a passive approach to learning is a red herring: film can be used to get pupils to think. It may be true that many films are unsuitable in terms of content and vocabulary. The solution is simply not to use those films; there is more than enough suitable material. Dramatic reconstructions can be biased and/or inaccurate. But spotting the bias/inaccuracies can be the main reason for viewing particular films. Pupils should be aware that film can easy lull one into a false sense of security and need to be trained to evaluate film critically. Asking key questions of film is often pleasanter and more effective than asking similar questions of other types of source.

We believe that films have the greatest influence when their content reinforces and extends previous knowledge. We also think there is often a good case for showing film extracts twice – the first time for impact, the second for discussion and reinforcement. We are certain that film is most effective when used by good teachers who put it in some kind of context, are ready to use clips and to 'freeze frame' at crucial points, and who tell the pupils what to look out for. Careful previewing is thus essential.

Visits

Museums, historic buildings and sites have, according to the HWG, 'an enormous potential for bringing history to life and creating a lasting impression on the pupils' (1990, p.178). We would not disagree with this or with the HWG's view that site visits should form an 'integral part of the school curriculum for history' (1990, p.177). There is massive potential. Since 1960 the number of museums in Britain has risen from 800 to over 2,000. English Heritage has over 350 monuments and historic buildings. Some sites are 'real', others go in for reconstructions. The purist might disapprove of some of the reconstructions. We quite like them – as do most pupils.

Although the local landscape varies enormously from one part of Britain to another, most places contain evidence of some aspect of human activity in the past. It is important that pupils understand that a historic environment is all around them. Often the lesser known part of our heritage is of greater educational potential than a famous site. Graveyards and war memorials, for example, have considerable school potential.

Many of the larger museums and sites have made great strides to improve the way they display and present history. Some have educational officers to help teachers plan school visits. Many places provide a range of resources for use on site and in the classroom. But it is very desirable for teachers to make preliminary visits to decide how they might use the site. It is often wise to select a part of a site for particular study and/or to allocate groups to various work-stations. If time permits, pupils can move from observation point to observation point, looking for clues and trying to set up hypotheses.

Whether a visit is best at the start, middle, or end of a topic is a moot point. We are of the view that it doesn't really matter providing teachers are clear about how the visit relates to what is being done in school.

Taking pupils 'into the field' to see places and items of a historical nature can give them a sense of the atmosphere of the past, help them empathise, test their deductive skills, and increase their enthusiasm for history. The fact that museums and sites provide 'concrete' and three dimensional evidence can, some claim, help make history more understandable to pupils.

However, there is a negative side to all of this. Visits can be expensive, time consuming and disrupt the school timetable. Moreover, the belief that a visit automatically gives youngsters a better understanding might be mistaken. Pond (1983) pointed out that pupils sometimes experience considerable difficulty seeing beyond the here and now of the situation, even when there has been solid preparation within the context of a carefully planned programme of work. He argued that they find it hard to distinguish on the basis of observation between 'what is' and 'what was' and suggests that although we think we are helping pupils by giving them 'concrete' experiences, we could in reality be making things more difficult. Pupils tend to see what is immediately perceptible. Pond's views are a warning that visits to historic sites are not a cure-all and that we should not assume children will understand simply because they have seen.

Artefacts

Sometimes, rather than pupils visiting a site to see artefacts, it is possible for artefacts to 'visit' schools. Some museum services provide loan services while pupils can often bring in 19th and 20th century artefacts from home. Artefacts are more used at Key Stages 1 and 2 than at Key Stages 3 and 4. This is unfortunate. Objects from the past are often a good introduction to a topic, giving pupils a real 'feel' for the past. John West's Dudley Project (1981) had primary age children working in groups handling and discussing artefacts, and this strategy can work just as well with secondary pupils. Interrogating artefacts through a series of questions – Is it authentic? What is it made from? Do we have things like this nowadays? What was it used for? Who would have used it? How old is it? – help pupils to use them as evidence.

Information technology

Over the last decade there has been considerable growth in the use of IT in education. This is certain to continue. According to a recent NCET document, 'We are on the brink of a decade of radical developments in technology. These developments are so fundamental that they will alter our work, our culture and our educational systems.' (NCET 1994, p.i). Cynics among the history fraternity (of whom there are many) could – rightly – claim that they have been told this kind of thing many times before. If IT was so good, most history teachers would be using it. As it is, and as we write, IT is used only minimally by history teachers. There are several reasons for this. Firstly, the difficulty of access to school micros; secondly, expense; thirdly, conservatism, compounded by the fact that many history teachers lack confidence in working with micros; and fourthly, IT upsets normal classroom routines and can test teachers' organisational powers and classroom control. Just as it is clear that pupil IT work serves little purpose unless it is sustained by regular access, so teacher enthusiasm is dissipated unless regular use is made of IT.

But in many respects the micro is tailor-made for history learning, largely because it can be programmed to store, sort and retrieve large amounts of information at high speed. Freed from manually processing information, pupils can concentrate on interpreting and using data.

IT will grow in value as more powerful computers offer greater ease of use, more powerful analysis, better graphic facilities, and greater storage capacity. CD-ROM's potential is already apparent. One disk can typically hold the equivalent of 300,000 pages of text and can also store and display images (still and moving) and CD quality sound. There are some tremendous CD-ROM programs already on the market. For example *World War II Archives* (Attica Cybernetics Limited), produced in conjunction with the Imperial War Museum, contains a wealth of primary material, including over 500 photographs and pieces of wartime art, over three hours of sound, 30 minutes of film, government archives, Cabinet papers, etc.

As well as helping learners to research and question, micros can also be used to run simulations (see below) and for word-processing.

Micros can give pupils more control over their own learning. Working at their own speed, pupils can try out ideas, receive immediate positive feedback and learn from their mistakes without the fear of ridicule. The micro, like all other resources, needs to be used with some discrimination. It certainly does not make teachers redundant: they need to be ready to intervene to encourage or reinforce learning when the micro is being used. But there is no doubt that IT can make a significant contribution to history. There is no doubt as well that history can make a significant contribution to the delivery of IT in the curriculum.

Simulation

History HMI have long been convinced that simulation techniques are 'a good thing'. However, there is plenty of evidence to suggest that history teachers have been oblivious, even resistant, to using such methods. Many hard-headed professionals claim that such methods simply do not work. Such views should not simply be dismissed. Simulation is not as easy or necessarily as effective as some of its supporters imply. That said, we do favour its use.

Before considering the potential of simulation we need to make clear our terminology. We regard the word simulation as an over-arching term and see the following distinct types:

1. Games – games have clear rules and involve competition.

2. Case study – here a situation, real or imaginary, is described and the participants are asked to discuss what they might or might not do. A case study can be an individual or group activity but does not involve drama.

3. Role play – this is different from a case study in that it involves an element of drama and is not 'static': there must be some improvisation and some interaction between participants. But it is more structured than free drama and has more specific objectives, often involving decision making.

4. Open drama – participants do their 'own thing', although greater benefits can be had by imposing constraints within which they have to work.

5. Controlled drama – here we have in mind drama based on written scripts.

6. Computer simulation – computer simulations can be games, case studies or role plays. In these, all the elements of the problem/situation under investigation are resolved into mathematical formulae and the resulting exercise is largely a solution of various equations.

Unfortunately, things are not quite as clear cut as the above suggests. Simulations are often hybrid activities, a mix of game/case study, or case study/role play, or role play/free drama. However, we do wish to stress that there are massive differences between some types of simulation (for example, free drama and computer simulation). Each type of simulation has its own particular advantages and disadvantages and some types are, arguably, more effective than others. Some types appeal to some learners. Some do not! It is difficult, therefore, to generalise about simulation methods.

The case for simulation

Relatively little has been written about simulation in history teaching. Birt and Nichol's book, *Games and Simulations in History* (1975) remains the only work which tackles the issue in some depth. (The authors, as the title of their book indicates, see little difference between games and simulations.) They list six major advantages arising from gaming (i.e. simulation!) activity. These are:

1. Motivation – games are a positive stimulus: the students become more enthusiastic and this enthusiasm spills over into other parts of the course.

2. Empathy – simulations help students 'understand and appreciate points of view different from their own'. They are a means by which pupils are 'drawn into a form of understanding and an insight into character and motivation which might otherwise be denied them' (1975, p.6).

3. Insight into the historical process – simulations enable teachers to demonstrate the multiplicity of possible outcomes of any historical situation and give pupils a new insight into the historical process.

4. Learning and recall – the acting out of roles and the active handling of historical materials enables pupils more easily to recall the topic concerned.

5. Social skills – much historical simulation activity takes place in small groups. Group activity encourages co-operation between pupils, fosters increased social skills, and helps increase pupils' fluency in using ideas and information. Birt and Nichol thought this a particularly useful technique for mixed ability forms where the more able can help the less able but where all the pupils can contribute something.

6. Variety – simulation is often a new element in the classroom and variety is the spice of history teaching.

These specific justifications for using simulation techniques in history can be backed up by more general justifications. Simulation techniques for example, are clearly consistent with the idea of the teacher as facilitator, creating learning opportunities and managing learning resources, rather than as the 'fount of all wisdom'. They are also consistent with the view that pupils should take a more active role in their own learning and with ideas about helping learners to see history 'from within'.

The case against simulation

Most of Birt and Nichol's claims for simulation can be countered:

1. Motivation – simulations do not necessarily motivate. There can be considerable initial consumer resistance and also a distinct fall in class interest once the honeymoon period is over.

2. Empathy – there is no hard evidence that simulations do encourage the development of empathy.

3. Insight into the historical process – this clearly depends on the simulation. If the simulation is inaccurate then little of value will come out of it. History, by definition, is about the unique and particular. Attempts at simulation model building may grossly over-simplify/distort/make unreal the historical process.

4. Learning and recall – although there has been considerable research into the effectiveness of simulation methods, there is little evidence to suggest that pupils do gain significantly more knowledge or understanding as a result of using such methods.

5. Social skills – pupils do not necessarily acquire social skills as a result of simulation. (It is difficult to see precisely what social skills a student working individually on a computer simulation is acquiring!) Students have a host of different learning styles. Some enjoy role play and group activities, but others find such work positively upsetting and contribute little.

6. Variety – if simulation methods are used to excess, they can become as dull as any other teaching method used continuously. Some simulations take a long time to 'play' and become dull as a result.

Other, more general, claims for simulation work can also be challenged, although debate is difficult in the absence of research-based evidence.

Those teachers who favour simulations also face serious practical problems, which are common to many active history teaching methods:

1. Class management problems – far from simulation being the key to good control, good control is usually the key to good simulation work. There is always the danger of role play/free drama sessions descending into chaos.

2. An added workload – simulation sessions can require more preparatory work than formal lessons. The actual running of a role play or free drama session also makes considerable demands on a teacher.

3. Expense – good simulations can be expensive to buy.

4. Previewing – it is very difficult to know whether you are getting value for money without previewing a simulation, and this can pose problems. Some are not readily available for inspection and inspecting the ones that are is not an easy business. Neither reading the instructions nor inspecting the materials can necessarily reveal the flow of interactions which may occur in practice.

5. Numbers – often only small numbers can fully participate in a simulation.

6. Timetable constraints – suitable rooms are not always available. Moreover many simulations take a long time to play and do not easily fit into regimented periods.

7. Availability – this is a major constraint. On the surface there is a plethora of simulations available, but unfortunately many fall between two stools. Some are far too simple. Complex issues are reduced to simple either/or choices and there is little scope for individual skill or thought beyond shaking a dice or pressing a keyboard letter. Other simulations are far too complex. We are thinking here of many of the strategic and military games which Oppenheim (1982) recommended in his article 'Complex Games and Simulations in School'. It might be true that every conceivable battle from David and Goliath to the Gulf War can be fought on boards but most of these war games are totally unsuitable for use with the vast majority of classes. The only 'intellectual' board game which we have found workable in a classroom is *Diplomacy*. This tries to recreate the situation pre-1914 and players control one of seven countries, aiming to make themselves (by diplomacy and shrewd movements of armies and navies) the strongest nation in Europe. This can arouse and sustain interest and, with some adjustment, can be fitted into a double session. But even *Diplomacy* has its problems. There are only seven countries so players have to be doubled up or several *Diplomacy* sets purchased. Moreover, the game is about as realistic a representation of the years after 1900 as chess is a simulation of a medieval battle. *Diplomacy* is essentially an enjoyable game – little more.

8. Interest – some simulations designed for school use (for example, *Longman History Games*) tend to be dull, too lengthy and often difficult to manage.

The work of Jordan and Wood

All is not gloom and doom. Over the last two decades two simulation enthusiasts, Chris Jordan and Tim Wood, have produced some good history material, especially of the investigative role play variety. Their ideas are available in several forms.

They have produced several textbooks – for example, *England in the Middle Ages* and *The Modern World* – containing a variety of types of simulations. *The Modern World*, for example, contains a complex but workable game, *The Cuban Missile Crisis 1962*, in which pupils play the part of Khruschev and the Russians or the part of American Presidents Eisenhower and Kennedy. It's designed to be played after pupils have learned something about the Cold War but before they know anything about the Cuban missile crisis. Knowledge of the event will tend to spoil the game.

They also produced the *History Action Packs* series for Arnold (now Hodder). These include *The Roman Empire*, *The Vikings*, *The Black Death*, *Medieval Medicine*, *The Spanish Armada* and *Slavery*.

Some of these are games (*Slavery* has its own board game). Others, for example *The Black Death*, are investigative role plays. *Medieval Medicine* is a mixture of game and role play and is probably the best thing Jordan and Wood have yet devised. We have seen it operate in many different situations and have never seen it fail. It aims to show pupils the work of the medieval doctor and the plight of medieval patients. Pupils are divided into doctors and patients. Each doctor is given a cure. The doctors' aim is to sell their cures to as many patients as possible, using all their powers of persuasion. They keep a record of the patients who buy their cures. The winning doctor is not just the one who sells the most cures. Extra points can be won by selling cures to patients who are likely to benefit from the cure.

The 'patients' have a variety of illnesses. Their task is to visit the doctors, describe their symptoms, listen to the doctors' prescriptions and then decide which cures will prove best for their particular complaint.

The simulation is easy to operate. Doctors sit in different parts of the classroom and the patients move about, discussing their problems and deciding on their cures. The activity lasts from 30 minutes to an hour depending on the motivation of the class.

At the end of the simulation, the teacher, using information which comes with the Pack, reads out the points earned by patients for each cure according to illness. The points are based on modern medical opinions of medieval treatments. The teacher should explain what each of the illnesses was and why some cures were more successful than others. The teacher also needs to stress that some of the 'cures', such as blood-letting and sipping mercury, could be lethal while others, such as charms, might have considerable psychological value in certain cases. This can lead on to discussion of alternative medicine today. The teacher also needs to point out that some patients, for example those with bubonic plague, stood no chance whatsoever!

Tim Wood also produced a series, P*layback: History Roleplays* (1982), containing five 18th and 19th century role plays. These are *The Burning of Mr Swan's Factory in 1812*; *Jackson's Mill: 1830 Factory Conditions*; *Hertson Prison: 1780*; *Broad Street: 1854* (A cholera investigation!) and *Westford Workhouse: 1842*.

These are aimed at pupils between the ages of 13 and 17. Each contains:

- An introduction which sets the scene and explains the purpose of the inquiry.
- Evidence which is usually in the form of original extracts and/or pictures or maps. The evidence is kept to a minimum but it is always important to the inquiry and is intended to act as a starting point for the questions.
- Detailed roles for the various witnesses to be cross-examined.
- A selection of tasks, designed to consolidate the work the pupils have done and to widen the inquiry.

Teachers need to choose the 'witnesses' carefully and ensure they are well primed. Their performances will make or break the role play. Teachers can either be neutral chairpersons, suggesting fruitful lines of enquiry and pulling various threads together, or they can take one of the crucial roles. Either way they must ensure that important ideas are not missed.

Wood suggests that his role plays are best used as introductions to topics, stimulating pupils to do the necessary follow-up work. He points out that if a topic is taught first, the impact of the witnesses will be lost.

The work of Wood and Jordan is seminal – although John Nichol and Bernard Barker should also be mentioned in despatches. Many of Nichol's best simulations appeared in the *Evidence* series published by Blackwell. Barker produced a *History Replay* series which attempted to recreate the complexities of a number of 20th century events.

And that is about it! Little else, computer simulation apart, has been published over the last two decades.

Do it yourself?

Given that there are so few ready-made simulations available, it has sometimes been suggested that teachers should produce their own. 'Pies or games: home made is best', wrote Elliott, Sumner and Waplington in the *Place, Time and Society* 8–13 booklet *Games and Simulations in the*

Classroom (1975, p.9). This is a catchy slogan – and little more. The general tips given by the *Place, Time and Society* team (and by Birt and Nichol) are largely unhelpful; a few platitudes which give the misleading impression that the process is simple. More useful pieces – Jones (1980) and Twelker (1977) – point out the difficulties of the process. In Twelker's view there are few workable guidelines for simulation design that are 'truly meaningful to the layman that enable him personally to design a simulation whether he be an elementary schoolteacher or a college professor.' (1977, p.13). Even if there were such guidelines, teachers would still need the creative spark and then the stamina to produce a finished product. The average role play, in Jones's view, takes about one hundred hours to design!

Case studies, it should be said, are neither expensive nor time consuming to produce (they are often found in good textbooks) and can be used to achieve a wide variety of objectives in terms of both content and process. One problem is deciding precisely how much information pupils need: too much information can be as bad as too little. Another is that case studies are not always very appealing: they are simply textbook/worksheet tasks.

Computer simulations

Computer simulations cannot be produced by ordinary or even extraordinary history teachers. There is a growing number of – often very expensive – programs on the market. What criteria should history teachers use when thinking about purchasing them? We suggest:

1. Programs should be simple and straightforward with clear instructions both on screen and in the instruction manual.

2. Programs should be historically authentic.

3. They should encourage children to ask historical questions, make decisions based on considerations of evidence and enable them to increase their knowledge.

4. Programs should encourage empathy.

5. Programs need to be compatible with a department's scheme of work. The length of time needed to use a simulation can be crucial. (A good IT simulation, of course, might determine a school's scheme of work!)

6. A good program allows pupils to experience something normally impossible in a classroom situation.

7. It needs to be attractive in format. Colour and good graphics are likely to stimulate initial interest, often crucial in determining whether a program is successful.

8. The program should have suitable back-up resources.

Some IT simulations such as Tressell's *Attack on the Somme* work successfully in the classroom. Some, for example Tressell's *1665* which asks pupils to make informed decisions about what to do in the plague-hit London of 1665, are tremendously conceived. But many, as is the case with *1665*, take too long to run. And some, quite simply, are a waste of money. Problems with IT simulations do not end there, for most of the general problems with simulations manifest themselves with IT-based simulations.

Drama

Drama is another type of simulation activity which can enrich the historical experience. We are not convinced there is much to be said for the type of drama where children read or mime set historical parts, so we will not say it! Open drama, however, can be an opportunity for pupils to reconstruct the past imaginatively. Costumes and scenery are not essential. Far more important is the confidence of the teacher and his/her belief in the activity. It is essential that the topic on which the children are going to be let loose is well introduced. Thereafter, it is best to give the pupils freedom to plan and generate ideas, while intervening to introduce problems and constraints which require them to consider carefully the perspectives of the characters they are playing. The teacher also needs to intervene to clarify muddled thinking and to feed in useful historical information.

Unfortunately few history teachers are drama specialists. There are many specific drama skills which take time to learn and time to use in a crowded curriculum. Many teachers are apprehensive of giving the pupils too much free rein and risking losing control. Also, good drama is not necessarily good history. However, those who have the requisite skills should use them. Court scenes and public enquiries are potentially rich areas for the use of drama in history.

It is a good idea to use a video camera to record drama and role play activity. This usually motivates pupils to prepare efficiently and sensibly, and most enjoy seeing themselves after the event. The teacher can use the recording as a valuable part of the debriefing exercise which should follow every type of simulation.

Other activities for gaining historical information

There are a number of other methods, not simulations as such but often regarded as 'active' because they involve group work. These include:

Brainstorming

Give groups of pupils the task of listing anything that comes to mind about a new topic. For some reason this works best if pupils have large sheets of paper and bold pens.

Broken information exercises

Pupils are divided into groups. Each group is given pieces of information, presented separately on cards and shared out randomly (but roughly equally) among the group members – usually three or four cards each. The information on the cards, if shared, provides a solution to a problem. Each group is told that their task is to arrive at the correct solution to the problem. Pupils can communicate orally but must not exchange cards or show them to anyone else. It is possible to throw in cards which are red herrings – useless pieces of information, designed to take groups up the wrong path! The aim of the exercise is to test learners' problem-solving abilities and to encourage oral participation by every group member.

Video news

Groups are required to produce a five minute radio or TV news broadcast using information supplied by the teacher. For example the groups might be given material from 3 September 1939 or 6 June 1944. The news items (usually taken from old newspapers) are fed to them gradually, right up to the time they go on air. The groups can rewrite material and interview members of their own team in various roles, but must not invent news. It is important that every group member should be involved in some way. The broadcast is finally recorded either on tape or video.

Activities that are useful for working on historical information

Chart completion

Charts are an effective way of summarising a large amount of information in a form that is easy to scan and easy to mark.

A classic example is the pyramid that summarises the relationships within the Feudal System, and flow charts showing, for example, the processes of steel are also quite common. Teachers have the opportunity to take these charts, white out parts of them and ask learners to fill in the blanks, or to produce a blank chart and get learners to complete it. The example in Table 3.1 is organised around the concepts of change and continuity. Learners complete it individually or in pairs towards the end of their study of the Tudors and Stuarts. They then 'pyramid' into larger groups with the brief of discussing their several versions of the chart and producing a group version. These are in turn pooled and discussed and a master chart is produced and printed off for the whole class.

Aspect of C16 and C17 life	Situation about 1500 AD	Situation about 1700 AD
Royal power	King limited by custom and the need to get consent for taxes	
Parliamentary power		Parliament is a regular feature of government, but it still does what the monarch wants
The Church		
Women's lives		

Table 3.1 An extract from a chart completion exercise

The chart can be made easier by including fewer categories, providing some answers, providing a list of points from which learners can choose and by giving references to places where relevant information may be found. It might be made harder by getting learners to add their own categories or by asking that they identify instances of continuity and of change for each category. The same principles apply for other charts, such as one summarising the causes of the Peasants' Revolt (general and specific causes?), five key events, reasons for its success and consequences of it (long and short term?). Maps (showing the pace of expansion, the spread of innovations, the course of a battle) can also be annotated using the same principles.

Flow charts

These are a variant of chart completion activities and can be used like 'fill in the blanks' questions to see whether learners understand a process, or learners can be asked to summarise their understanding by making a chart to show the several stages in a process. They are much easier for teachers to mark than the traditional set of notes or essay. A rather crude chart, which has been partly completed, is shown in Table 3.2.

The domestic system of cloth making

---

1. Sheep raised by farmer (if the farmer also spins and weaves, go to 5 below).

2. Sheep sheared. Fleece bought by wool merchant.

3. Fleeces washed, dried and carded (combed ready for spinning).

4. Wool merchant has wool sent to outworkers for spinning and weaving.

5.

6. Wool woven on hand loom.

7. Merchant collects cloth, paying the workers according to how much they've done and how well they've done it.

8. Cloth dyed.

9.

10. Some cloth sold for home-made clothing; some sold to tailors (who would buy the clothes they made?); much is exported.

Question: Who do you think made the most money out of this system?

Table 3.2 A flow chart completion exercise

Correct the mistakes

This is a serviceable way of establishing how well learners have grasped certain information. It is often regarded as a low-level activity, which is a fair reflection on tasks such as:

> ### Underline the mistakes
>
> The Beale Street Crash of 1928 bought America to its feet...
> (four mistakes).

A more powerful variant would go something like this (although the version we use in class is longer):

> *In this summary of the Wall Street Crash of 1929 there are three statements that I think we can argue about. First, underline any of these statements that you can find. Then work in groups of three to produce a group answer, which we will talk about.*
>
> The Wall Street Crash of 1929 brought America to its knees. Companies collapsed, some businessmen killed themselves and unemployment rocketed. The main cause was Hoover's poor handling of the economy. The effects hit all Americans and led to unemployment on a scale that we have never seen. It took the genius of Franklin Delano Roosevelt, elected in 1933, to solve the problems, which he did in his first hundred days.

Yes, there are more than three disputable statements – that adds to the power of this task for getting a class to think about their grasp of the Great Depression.

The key point is that this exercise sparks off discussion about the materials that pupils have accumulated, leading them to shape awarenesses in line with informed historical opinion.

Diamond factor ranking

This is a very powerful device for ranking the importance of things – changes, causes, and effects, for example. We start with a list of the things to be ranked – in Figure 3.1 reasons for the French Revolution. Each reason is put on a card (teachers may make their own sets of cards or, perhaps better still, get learners each to produce four 'reasons' cards). Each pair or group is given a selection of cards and asked to sort them into a diamond shape.

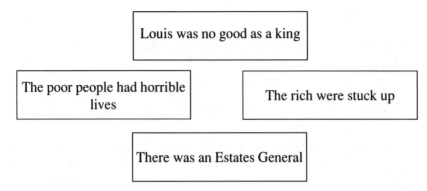

Figure 3.1 The form of a diamond factor ranking exercise

In this case they have been asked to make a diamond four, putting the most important cause at the top, the two next most important causes second, and the fourth most important on the bottom row. The principle can be extended to a diamond nine (with 1, 2, 3, 2 and 1 cards per row), which makes it much harder.

Groups are then joined together to produce composite diamonds which form the basis for discussion – and in this case discussion is desperately needed.

Drawing

We have mentioned one example of a valuable drawing task but our general tone has been sniffy. Yet, there is value to drawing where two conditions can be met. First, it should not take a disproportionate amount of time and second, it should be valuable as history work, rather than as decoration and recreation.

Strip cartoons can be a good and enjoyable way of getting learners to summarise a sequence and tell a story. The cartoon convention makes it accessible to the less literate, as well as offering an interesting variant on 'write about King John'. Constraint can be added by requiring that the cartoon take no more than, say, six or eight frames which forces learners to think about the most important features of the story or sequence. A word of advice. Tell the cartoonists that the way to do speech bubbles is to write the words first and then surround them with the bubble.

A second type of drawing asks learners to represent a person or a scene from a specific point of view. Again, a cartoon style may be appropriate for trying to portray Louis XVI as a satirical pamphlet might have seen him, or the *sans culottes* as the surviving nobility might have thought of them.

Fill in the blanks

This is an old standby. Often used as a way of summarising work that has been done, it requires relatively little thought and can easily and undetectably be copied. To some extent these problems can be relieved by providing a list of words to be used that is greater than the number of blanks to be filled and by leaving longer blanks that require learners to add a complete clause.

Perhaps it is better to use a 'fill in the blanks' exercise as a way of guiding encounters with new material. Not only would this structure the reading (ideally from more than one book), but it would also provide a ready-made set of notes about it.

Mix and match

This is a very simple type of task that can be used to encourage more or less demanding activity. First, a 'stems and tails' variant to get learners to review their knowledge of the Middle Ages is shown in Table 3.3.

Match each statement in the left hand column with the words in the right hand column that make a complete sentence. Do this by drawing a line to join each pair.

The Feudal System was where	that they brought a motte and bailey castle with them.
King Harold was killed by an arrow through the eye	– allegedly!
The Saxons lost at Hastings because	each person served the person above them and got protection and land in return.
Evidence that the Normans were well-prepared for an invasion is	they lacked discipline.

Table 3.3 A mix and match exercise

Mix and match can also be used more creatively to get at more demanding ideas (Table 3.4).

Match each statement in the left hand column with the words in the right hand column that make a complete sentence. Do this by drawing a line to join each pair. There are more things in the right hand column than the left – do not use them all.

History is about	people.
Change is sometimes	is a part of the reason why it happened.
	from change, some don't.
Change is not the same as	fast, sometimes slow.
Some people benefit	books.
	is its cause.
What happens just before an event	progress.

Table 3.4 A mix and match exercise on the nature of history

Graph making

This, too, is a well-worn activity, particularly useful in giving numbers some visual impact. In many classrooms graphs are often printed out directly from computer databases, which supports historical analysis of the data without bogging it down in the tedium of drawing graphs by hand. Where this option is not available, it makes sense for the teacher to prepare and print the base grids and there is a case for actually drawing the graph too (*especially* if a pie graph is wanted) and leaving the learners to label it and discuss and apply the data.

When it comes to interpreting graphs showing change over time it is helpful for learners to know that we can look at the difference between two points or bars to see the *amount* of change (the increase in population between 1831 and 1891, for example) but we need to look at the gradient to see when the *rate* of change was greatest – the steeper the gradient, the greater the rate of change.

Judging value of sources

Learners need to understand the difference between evidence and information, superfluity and sources if they are to have much grasp of history's procedures. The value of sources has to be judged against their usefulness as evidence in response to a specific question, so there can be no general task on judging the value of sources: it must always be done within a context. Figures for the population of Barrow-in-Furness are hardly helpful if we want to know about living conditions, although they are of some help if we want to know how important a place it was. Data from the 1851 census are much better, since we can see how many people lived in different sorts of houses.

We suggest two main types of activity. One comes early in the study of a topic. Learners are asked what kinds of sources might give information on a variety of themes. For example:

Below is a set of questions. Against each question, write two types of source which you think might help us to answer it.

1. What did Tudor peasant women do?

2. How important was religion in the lives of the poor?

3. Were people happy in Tudor England?

4. What did they do when they got ill?

A variant is for learners to generate their own list of questions that they would like to answer in the course of a topic and then to go on and imagine sources that might be of use.

A second approach directs learners to sources that they have used and asks them to evaluate their value in respect of specific enquiries (see Table 3.5).

Below there is a list of sources that you have used. The question is which is the most useful as evidence about the Battle of Hastings. In the right hand column there are some comments. Draw lines to link each source with the comments that go with it.

The Bayeux Tapestry	Tells you what historians think happened. A helpful summary.
The Anglo-Saxon Chronicle	Useful – it's nearly contemporary, but how biased is it?
Excavations at Senlac Hill	Well, it's fun to read but why should we trust her?
William of Poitiers' account	Written after the event and based on hearsay.
Medieval England, by T. Past and T. Present.	Useless!
	Tells us there was a battle there.
William the Bastard (a modern novel) by B. Wagonfield	We don't know when it was written but there's no reason to disbelieve it.

Table 3.5 A structured source appraisal exercise

We could also use diamond ranking and ask learners to explain the reason why they have chosen one source as the most valuable.

Making timelines

There is little to say here beyond the obvious point that learners need to use timelines in history, much as they use maps in geography; and that it's important not to clutter them with too much detail and dates. Making timelines to show the key events in, say, Stuart England or the main technical innovations of the late 18th Century is a useful revision activity.

Map search

Maps are much used in history but not properly exploited. We do need maps to show where Marco Polo went, or where Czechoslovakia is, but we can base more active learning on them.

Suppose that we are doing work on the indigenous people of North America. Using relief, climate and vegetation maps we can find out a great deal about an area (perhaps Virginia, where the first Stuart colonists settled). From that we might make guesses about the way of life of the native people and certainly raise awkward questions about the assumption that Amerindians looked like leftovers from a John Wayne film. Similar activities lie behind work on the location of settlements and industry, on trade routes and on warfare. In no case is the map evidence sufficient, but in most cases it is a useful source of ideas that can be tested against available evidence, often showing the good geographical sense behind what people did in the past.

Parallels

Parallels are a provocative thinking device, although they depend on learners actually recalling quite a lot of history, which may not always be a realistic thing to expect. The principle is closely related to the ideas discussed at the end of the previous chapter. An example, based on a study of a non-European society, is shown in Table 3.6.

We have been looking at the Mexica (Aztecs) and know quite a lot about them. How do they compare with the people of England at that time? Try and complete the following table: For each thing, try to spot one way in which they were like each other and, if it's important, a way in which they differed.

Area of focus	Tudor England	The Mexica c.1520
The ruler		
Religion		
etc.		

Table 3.6 An extract from a structured comparison exercise

We might do the same for revolutions (the English, French and Russian); for the impact of the development of new sources of energy; for different sources (census returns, parish registers, electoral rolls and graveyard evidence); or for life before and after a development (i.e. before and after the Norman Conquest). As ever, the greatest value comes in the follow up work, where one might be asking about the degree to which change was evident, or the value of different sources for an enquiry, or the extent to which revolutions are similar in cause and nature. One way of reducing the substantial demands on learners' existing historical awareness is to give them brief notes, charts or summary sketches to remind them of key elements of some of the points of comparison.

Post-its

Post-its are those sticky, yellow labels. Each learner or group of learners can be given a few and asked to write on them. The labels can then be collected, redistributed and learners asked to arrange them in a given pattern. For example:

> Work by yourself. List all the sources that might be helpful if we wanted to find out about everyday life in Coketown c.1891. Write down one thing that each source might tell us about. Each source should be written on a separate post-it.

> They will be collected in and a selection will be given to each group. Your job, as a group, is (a) to sort them into two groups, primary and secondary sources (use a highlighter to mark the secondary sources) and (b) to arrange them on a large sheet of paper in the form of a flow chart showing the order in which you would use these sources to find out about everyday life in old Coketown. Against each post-it, say why you would use this source — what questions might it help you to answer?

Sequencing extracts

Some sequencing activities are well known – for example, using the British Museum postcards of the Luttrell Psalter to show the sequence of the medieval farmer's year. More complicated – and demanding – work might present learners with a set of extracts from primary sources, complemented by some statistics, on public health in the mid-19th century and ask them to suggest the order in which they may have been written. We would include a 'rogue source', written in the 1880s and still complaining about poor sanitation, in order to make the point that change is not an all-or-nothing matter, but something that proceeds unevenly and sometimes slowly.

Sorting

We have already suggested several sorting activities. At the core is the idea of set theory, that is to say the idea that objects can belong to one set or another, or, sometimes, to both. Take a collection of photographs of the 1930s, for example. These could have been selected around the theme of fascism and parliamentary democracy. Some – pictures of Hitler, Kristallnacht, book burning, a newspaper report of the invasion of Czechoslovakia – are clearly to do with fascism. Others, showing elections, people at work, housing, or leisure are more problematic and will often not fit well with one set or the other, while a picture of the hustings or of hunger marches fits the UK better than Italy or Germany. This fuzziness is deliberate and should lead to the powerful question: what was the main difference between parliamentary democracy and fascism?

A set of pictures might show violent revolution in the 20th century as well as the more subtle revolution in living standards. Learners might be asked to sort out those which they see as illustrative of the concept of revolution, which should lead to discussion of the concept itself.

Tabulating

Some of the tasks that we have reviewed so far ask learners to complete tables to summarise their understandings. We want to make the point formally that this can be a powerful task for active history. Suppose we are interested in the impact of changes in public health between 1800 and 1900. Table 3.7 might help to direct thinking on the issue.

The left hand column shows some of the things that the Victorians did to improve public health. Did all people benefit from them? You might find it helpful to keep the extracts from the Report of the Sanatory Condition of Lancaster beside you as you fill in the table. (It shows how town and country conditions differed.)

	Middle class in towns	Middle class in the countryside	Workers in towns	Workers in the countryside
Pure water supply to towns				
Sewer schemes in major towns				
Provision of public parks				

Table 3.7 A tabulation exercise

Pulling history together

Learners have to make sense of any new experience before their knowledge of it is really useful to them. Knowledge reformulated by the learner is more easily recalled and an aid to further learning. Sometimes all this happens without the teacher having to worry about it. It happens at home or quietly in the minds of pupils who might seem to be just passively listening. But teachers must assist the process. Active teaching involves encouraging and provoking the sorts of talking, writing and reading tasks that will help the making-sense process.

Before considering the types of tasks which help pupils reformulate material, seven points need to be made:

1. The struggle to communicate what you want to say is one of the most powerful ways of sorting out what you understand. Unfortunately many pupils have terrible difficulty in re-expressing ideas for themselves, especially in writing. Their failure to achieve and be motivated results in teachers giving more and more to them and demanding less and less of them. This is understandable but defeatist. We reiterate that without some element of intelligent engagement and challenge, pupils' historical understanding is unlikely to develop.

2. Getting pupils to use language well is not just a matter of having a set of techniques. The context in which these techniques are used – and especially the relationship between teacher and pupil – is particularly important.

3. Pupils need to be set increasingly demanding activities as they grow in maturity and understanding. But it is often hard to say what makes a task harder or easier. Often it is simply the type of language used in asking pupils to do tasks. Setting tasks to fit the needs of pupils of varying aptitudes, and in particular breaking tasks down for less able pupils, is a key teaching skill.

4. Planning for differentiation needs to be tempered by realism. It is impossible to customise teaching and learning to meet all the individual needs of all pupils all the time. But there does need to be a wide variety of task-setting, allowing pupils to respond at a level suitable for their aptitude.

5. Many tasks can be done by Y7 or Y11 pupils but the expected outcomes might be very different.

6. Task-setting takes us deep into the assessment area. (This will be covered in more detail in Chapter 5.) Tasks are obviously set for a variety of purposes. Some are general – for example, to improve language development. But history teachers are also concerned with setting tasks

which enable pupils to display their understanding of particular skills or concepts. However, we do feel there is a danger of teachers setting too many source-based tasks, purporting to assess skills. Many of these tasks require five or six line answers. Such tasks, now the stock in trade of text book writers and GCSE examiners, can become boring for both teachers and pupils alike.

7. In the old National Curriculum there was no AT assessing pupils' ability to organise and communicate the results of historical study. There ought to have been!

Talk and discussion

Speaking is of immense potential value as a means to learning. Yet most classrooms are dominated by teacher talk. Discussion often means little more than question and answer in which, with the best will in the world, only a few pupils are ever directly involved. If talking is a 'good thing' – and it is vital for pupils who find reading and writing blocks to effective learning – then there is a need to use ways of working which allow pupils a chance for real talk.

The only way to get all pupils involved in the process is to organise group discussion activity. This is not as easy as it sounds. Many pupils are suspicious of oral work, seeing it as a soft option compared with the real work of reading and writing. Group discussion can quickly become an excuse for wasting time. It can also be caricatured as the blind leading the blind. The most vocal, not necessarily the most able, often dominate proceedings, while some shy pupils hate group work.

Nevertheless, be prepared to experiment and persevere with groups set up with the explicit purpose of discussing a prearranged topic. Group work does give pupils an opportunity to learn at their own level, to make sense of new information and to display what they know, think or have learned. 'Tips' for good group work include:

● Decide how the groups are to be selected – randomly, teacher choice or pupil choice. A case can be made for all three approaches. Much depends on a teacher's relationship with a particular class but it is usually best if the pupils do not select their groups.

● For many classrooms six is the maximum number of groups and five is often the best, one in each of the four corners and one in the middle. Five pupils per group also seems to be the magic number for group interaction. More than six and a group is too large; less than three and a group is hardly a group.

● Group tasks should be clearly structured and the topics should be sufficiently interesting to motivate pupils.

- Stimuli – in the form of artefacts, pictures, written sources, etc. – can ensure that pupils actually start talking.
- Set a time limit within which a task must be completed. Ten minutes is often more than sufficient!
- Allocate roles and responsibilities, for example chair, recorder, reporter.
- Monitor the various groups' progress and be prepared to intervene if they stray off target.
- Ask each group member to produce a short written piece at the end of the discussion, recording what he/she thinks was resolved by the group.

It is sometimes possible to move beyond group discussions. A class debate can work well, although this is often dependent on the skills of one or two pupils. We have found a more structured 'Question Time' format, where individuals represent particular people or groups, works better. For example, pupils could play the roles of a Nazi, a Nationalist, a Communist and a Social Democrat before the March 1933 election in Germany. The 'politicians' need to be well-primed beforehand. The rest of the class should come with questions they want to ask specific individuals or the panel as a whole.

Writing activities

It is essential that those who study history learn to write it. Unfortunately, many children have difficulty with writing. Too often it can become a form of less-than-subtle plagiarising, where pupils neither absorb nor really understand. It is possible to be negative and to say that learners' inability to write restricts the types of tasks which history teachers can set – which reduces pupils' ability to really understand history. But it is also possible to be positive and claim that history work provides a great opportunity for those who find writing difficult to develop their skills. This development is unlikely to occur if they are given an undemanding range of tasks and limited opportunities to write.

Whatever their age and ability, pupils should have the opportunity to express themselves in a variety of writing styles. This should include 'utilitarian' (or transactional) writing aimed at ensuring that they can write prose which is brief, logical, factual, relevant and accurate. It should also include writing with a creative emphasis in which pupils express their thoughts and feelings and cultivate their imaginations. As we shall show, pupils should also write for a range of audiences.

The essay

The essay has been the traditional form of examining history at all levels for decades. Although GCSE has played down its importance, the ability to write an essay remains a vital outcome of doing history. Essays encourage children to demonstrate the interrelationship of factors, to synthesise, to separate the trivial from the essential, to organise logically their thoughts and material, to argue and debate, to use evidence, and to handle facts correctly.

In order to develop essay-writing ability, stress the need for rough drafts rather than attempts to produce a finished product at one fell swoop. Teachers should also ensure that pupils experience a structured approach to essay writing. Providing them with paragraph headings is an important way of helping them develop their essay-writing skills.

Précis writing

Précis writing is an important skill which history should aim to develop. Getting learners to write a clear and concise paragraph describing an event or a character encountered in a book or lesson is a testing assignment.

Imaginative writing

There are many kinds of imaginative writing. These include:

- Writing a TV or radio script or play;
- Interviewing people from the past;
- Any of the forms encountered in journalism, for example letters to an editor, editorials, profiles of people, news stories with headlines (sometimes a collection of headlines is sufficient!), obituaries, reviews;
- Advert or poster making;
- Eye-witness accounts, for example letters home, diaries, ships' logs;
- Official reports, for example government reports, political broadcasts, military dispatches.

Imaginative tasks have their critics who claim that pupils are not sure whether to write a work of complete fiction or simply to recall the facts of the story. The finished products, it is argued, are usually factual pieces with an 'imaginative gloss' (Booth, Culpin and Macintosh, 1987, p.25). However, we tend to the view that many pupils find imaginative writing more enjoyable than transactional prose and writing that brings enjoyment is likely to increase engagement. Moreover, imaginative tasks can, we think, result in pupils displaying real historical understanding. The onus is on the teacher to provide ground rules and some structure so as to hinder the inclination to produce 'purple prose'.

Source-based written work

Much written work is based on answering questions raised by examining sources, usually written or visual but including maps, statistical data, charts and diagrams.

The kinds of questions asked of the sources vary considerably:

- Perhaps the easiest questions are the simple recall type.
- Beyond these are comprehension-type questions, testing whether pupils have a basic understanding of the source(s).
- Interpretation questions are more difficult. Pupils, for example, might be asked about the meaning or significance of a source.
- Comprehension and interpretation lead on to a consideration of the reliability and bias of sources. Pupils are encouraged to ask of all sources: Who produced it and for what purpose? When was it produced? Had the producer a particular axe to grind? Was (s)he present at the events described? Is the information reliable? How can we check?
- Extrapolation questions are usually seen as the hardest. Here pupils are asked to draw conclusions from the evidence and to create hypotheses, inferences and imaginative guesses. They must try to go beyond the information derived from the source(s), realising that inferences are not necessarily right or wrong and that there may be several possible answers.

Empathetic understanding can also be accessed by asking questions of sources: for example, what would you have thought or done in that person's position? Paradoxical – or unexpected – questions are regarded as particularly effective.

Several factors determine the level of difficulty of activities. These include the number and length and the type and complexity of the sources used, the nature of the events being studied, the nature of the groundwork leading up to source-based work, and the amount of help a teacher gives the pupils.

We are not against source-based questions. In many ways they are a better way of assessment than getting pupils to write four or five essays. But we do have two words of caution:

1. Pupils rarely encounter written sources in anything other than highly selective, very short extracts. This does not remotely approximate to the way historians use sources when conducting research. Moreover, umpteen short and contradictory sources can thoroughly bemuse less able pupils. Longer extracts give a better sense of the period from which they come and can often be used to better effect than a collection of short quotations.

2. We reiterate our fear that a surfeit of structured questions can be actually damaging and can restrict pupils' understanding of and interest in history.

Note-making

Note-making – whether copying notes from the board, taking them down in dictation or making notes from books – has long been regarded as one of the deadly sins of history teaching. Critics claim that note-making (and note-learning for exams/tests) spoiled history for many pupils and prevented real understanding. We have some sympathy with this view. Certainly note-making can be a barren activity and teachers should generally avoid dictating notes or simply getting pupils to copy from a board. That said, there are occasions when such methods do help classroom control and such notes can give pupils a good model for their own note-making. There are also occasions when pupils do need to be given material, if only to revise for exams. This can be done by distributing duplicated notes, but most pupils (and adults) learn more from their own notes than from those made by someone else.

Note-making can help pupils make sense of what they read or hear. The ability to make good notes is also an important skill which may well assist pupils in later life – at A level, in higher education and in many types of job. Perhaps it is facetious of us to suggest that if children are really to do what most historians spend much of their time doing, they would spend far more time making notes than beavering away on source-based tasks!

Making notes from a text is a particularly valuable activity. Pupils must extract the salient points, categorise and classify what they read, and express ideas concisely. Good note-making demands – and deepens – good understanding.

There is no single way of making notes. Most people prefer making linear notes: a few prefer 'branching' notes. Pupils need to develop a method to suit their own preferred way of working and they need to be given opportunities to do so. Pupils, for example, can be given short passages and asked to express the main ideas in them. They can be asked to write headings for paragraphs in textbooks. It is also worthwhile getting pupils to compare their note-making with that of other pupils. As with so many aspects of task and activity setting, life is made much easier when departments have adopted consistent policies throughout KS3 and 4 and when learners are systematically schooled in them.

Projects

The term 'project' is used to mean many different things in educational literature. Generally, however, a project is an investigation, by an individual or group, in which the participants are given some – and sometimes considerable – freedom in their choice of topic, mode of approach, and presentation of findings. Projects vary considerably in size and time allocated to them. There are two main types of investigatory projects in history:

1. Book-based – these make use of library sources, both within and outside the school.
2. 'Field'-based – these make use of local archives, the pupils' own family, or historic buildings and sites.

Pupil projects are a common form of assessment at GCSE although some examination boards prefer a batch of shorter pieces of work. A history project has many potential benefits:

- It can provide scope for original work.
- It can encourage pupils to do something similar to real historical research – selecting a topic, posing questions, identifying sources, collecting, recording and organising information, making judgements and drawing conclusions.
- By catering for individual interests and providing ample opportunity for greater initiative, it can be an important motivator.
- It can lend itself to and encourage co-operative group work.

However, there is a down side to project work:

- A history department needs considerable resources to support a wide range of lines of inquiry. Few schools have such resources.
- Fieldwork is expensive and it is sometimes hard to find realistic research topics related to resources which are locally available.
- Project work is a sophisticated activity and average or below average ability pupils may lack the necessary skills.
- Much project work simply involves pupils copying huge chunks from books.
- Projects do not necessarily make history more interesting: many pupils hate doing them.
- Teachers often find it hard to know how much assistance to give individuals or groups. Too much teacher help can destroy the point of a project. Too little help can result in disaster!

What makes for good project work?

- It is usually best if teachers exert some control by drawing up lists of possible topics, reducing freedom but ensuring that pupils do not embark on a disaster area.
- Teachers need to be enthusiastic and then efficient in planning and organising classes.
- Pupils should be clear that they need to pose a problem which they must then attempt to answer. A project should not be 'write all I know about...'
- Pupils should be aware from the start that they must ultimately report

their findings to the rest of the class. They can do this in a variety of ways: for example, prepare a booklet or create a display or video.

Drawing and three-dimensional work

Work does not always need to be written down. There are various tasks in history which do not involve (much!) writing but which can deepen under-standing. Such tasks are particularly good for motivating children who find it difficult to express themselves in writing – although we should not assume that such children are always good, for example, at drawing. But there are people of all abilities who find drawing and model-making a comfortable medium of expression, an enjoyable exercise and a means of gaining a real sense of achievement. Non-writing tasks in history include:

- Creating posters about an issue or event
- Making visual timelines
- Drawing a storyboard – the kind that a film producer might make – telling the story of an event in a set of eight to ten pictures (designing cartoon strips is a similar task)
- Making three-dimensional historical models.

Proponents claim that model-making can foster group co-operation and communication; provide an exercise in problem-solving; allow expression of historical understanding, especially if pupils have to consider the design as well as the construction of a model and work from historical sources to ensure that their models are reasonably authentic; and develop technolog-ical, artistic and practical skills.

However, we do have suspicions about such work. Most history teach-ers lack the necessary training to do first class art and craft work. They also lack specialist rooms and storage space, as well as time for preparation and clearing away. And the question must be asked: is what is being done really history? Constructing a model from a cut-out kit or commercial package will not provide pupils with great scope for problem-solving. The design of a basic cut-out model, on the other hand, would severely test the draughtsmanship of all but the most gifted pupils or history teachers! One of us has terrible memories of trying to get Year 7 pupils to build a motte and bailey castle. The task was unending, messy and had finally to be abandoned. This incident should not necessarily deter all teachers but it is a word of caution.

CHAPTER 4

Teaching Active History Through National Curriculum Core Units

In this chapter we suggest some ways in which teachers might approach actively planning and teaching the KS3 core units, two of which are also KS4 favourites. But first we need to make clear our thinking.

The new National Curriculum

The Dearing reforms, which are supposed to stand for five years, do not represent much of a scheme of work. For each of the four core units there is simply a block of content with relatively little shape or coherence. (The same was true of National Curriculum mark 1.) The key elements must also be taken into consideration. These state:

1. Pupils should be taught about the chronology of the main events and developments in the programme of study. They should be taught to use dates and terms relating to the passing of time, through which events are organised for the purposes of historical study.
2. They should be taught about features of particular periods or situations and the ways in which they are interrelated both within and across periods; about the social, cultural, religious and ethnic diversity of the societies studied; and about the experiences of men and women in these societies. They should be helped to analyse the ideas, beliefs and attitudes of different people in the past. Pupils should be given opportunities to describe, analyse and explain reasons for and results of the historical events, developments and changes studied.
3. They should see how and why some events, personalities or developments have been represented and interpreted in different ways.
4. They should learn how to find out about aspects of the periods studied, from a range of sources of information, including documents and

printed sources, artefacts, pictures and photographs, music, and buildings and sites; and ask and answer questions, and select and record
information relevant to a topic.

5. Pupils should recall, select and organise historical information, including
dates and terms; know the terms necessary to describe the periods and
topics studied; and communicate their knowledge and understanding of
history in a variety of ways, including structured narratives and
descriptions.

We have little but praise for the key elements though we do point out that
they are somewhat generalised platitudes. They inform: they certainly do
not dictate.

Schemes of work

We make the following points:

- What departments decide to teach will depend on a variety of factors:
the length of time allowed for history in the school; agreement within a
department about how much time is to be devoted to this unit; school
resources; local resources (for example, is there a castle, church or
monastery in the vicinity?); the interests and enthusiasms of teaching
staff; and whether there is differentiation within the classroom.

  It is thus impossible to provide a perfect scheme of work, and that is
not our intention. Our intention is simply to share our thoughts about
approaches to these core units. Some schools will cover some of our
topics in depth and cover others superficially – if at all.

- With any scheme of work there is a need to plan the unit as a whole so
that the scheme has some overall shape. This shape is often best determined by asking one or two over-arching and unifying questions. We
suggest that the National Curriculum Orders probably do provide the
over-arching questions.

- The main problem with any scheme of work is trying to fit the Pacific
Ocean into a pint glass. There is always far too much potential content
and never enough time to fit it all in. There is thus the danger of never
really completing a unit, or of covering some of the topics within a unit so
superficially that they are of little interest or value to the pupil. The only
solution is rigorous selection. *It is necessary to focus in depth on some
parts of the unit and cover other areas more quickly.* This is perfectly
legitimate: indeed it is, and always has been, part of good planning.

- Whenever possible we recommend that teachers use case studies of
individuals, events and places to illustrate and explain concepts. Most
pupils, for example, are more interested in individual medieval monarchs than they are in medieval monarchy as a concept. They are more

interested in Henry VIII than in the Reformation.

We would also encourage an investigative approach to most topics on the grounds that it is the essence of historical procedure and that it tends to motivate pupils.

- Planning any history unit must involve a partnership between content and assessment. However, we do not think that schemes of work should be assessment led. There is less need now for lessons in which a series of highly targeted questions focus on specific ATs or statements of attainment. But we do think that it is vital for departments to know what it is they are attempting to teach and to agree on common tasks which will aim to assess the level of pupils' knowledge, understanding and awareness of procedures. These tasks should involve a variety of approaches.

- We think that good schemes of work should not be too rigid. They should allow individual teachers to have some autonomy in terms of what they teach and how they assess.

- The old non-statutory guidelines (NCC 1991) provide several models for planning schemes of work. We prefer their basic matrix model which includes the following:

  - key themes, questions and hypotheses
  - concepts
  - content
  - resources
  - activities
  - teaching and learning methods
  - assessment
  - cross-curricular links.

The advantage of this layout is that it is highly focused on practical delivery and is easy to draw up.

Resources

Schemes of work and individual lessons depend upon school resources. We thought hard and long about whether to include a detailed section on resources in each of the following four sections on the core units. We finally decided against this idea for the following reasons:

- Many resources – and especially textbooks – soon date.
- Most of the resources we would list/recommend are already well known to most history departments. They are well advertised by publishers, TV companies, IT program producers, etc. They do not need us to advertise for them.
- It is difficult to recommend places to visit. Visits very much depend on

the locality of a school.

- It is difficult to recommend good video material for two reasons:
  - There is so much potential material available that it really is impossible to make any kind of comprehensive list, especially for the 20th century unit.
  - Much of the material we would recommend has been and gone and there is no guarantee that it will return. We don't think there is much point recommending material that isn't easily available. It is sometimes possible to buy good video material from retailers but this is far more expensive than recording from air. So we would simply recommend that teachers keep an alert weather eye for what programmes are on television from week to week, recording those which look as though they might be useful.

Lesson planning

Many factors influence lesson planning: the pupils themselves and their normal responses to teaching of different sorts; the time of day and week of the lesson; the availability of resources; etc.

Consequently, our aim is to provide a 'take your pick' selection of ideas. We have not generally assumed that schools have particular resources – although we do occasionally recommend some materials. We include little specifically in the way of sources or source-based tasks. Most recent text-books provide more than enough of both and we lack the space to compete. But we do assume that pupils will have plenty of primary and secondary sources available for use and will do a considerable number of source-based tasks. We do not suggest basic tasks like cloze exercises but nevertheless recognise that pupils will do such tasks.

Like all teachers, our ideas come from many sources and have been passed through the sieve of our classroom teaching. Many of them might be traced back to *this* book, to *that* colleague or to *those* classes. We apologise if some of our ideas are already familiar but we see no point in constantly reinventing (good) wheels.

We say little about assessment at this stage, for reasons which will become apparent in Chapter 5.

Medieval Realms

Overview

The 'Medieval Realms' unit has been slimmed down somewhat compared to its immediate precursor but there are no major differences between National Curriculum mark 1 and mark 2. The present 'rules' are that pupils should be introduced to the major features of Britain's medieval past. The focus should be on the development of the medieval monarchy and the way of life of the peoples of the British Isles. They should be taught about the following:

The development of the English medieval monarchy

- The Norman Conquest, including the Battle of Hastings and its impact;
- Relations of the monarchy with the Church, barons and people, including Magna Carta and other key events, for example *the Peasants Revolt (1381), the Wars of the Roses*;
- The involvement of English monarchs in Ireland, Scotland, Wales and France.

Medieval society

- The structure of medieval society, including the role of the Church, farming, crafts, towns and trade;
- Health and disease, including the Black Death;
- Arts and architecture.

This is a highly teachable unit and one which we think poses teachers relatively few problems. The unit seems to have been generally enjoyed.by both pupils and teachers and most schools now have good resources for it.

What follows are some suggestions for planning and teaching 'Medieval Realms' in an active way. We stress that our suggestions are merely starting points and that not all the topics we cover can be taught to the same depth. Schools must decide on the topics they intend covering in depth and those which they just intend 'visiting' (for example, by time-line).

The over-arching and unifying questions for this unit are likely to be:

- How did English medieval monarchy develop?
- What was English medieval society like?

Introducing the unit

We think it is a good idea to start with pupils brainstorming what they know about the situation in 1066 and perhaps the period as a whole. It might even be feasible to try to get them to produce a rough timeline. The question: 'how do we know?' follows on automatically and provides ample scope for discussion of the types of sources that have survived the 'shipwreck of time' and which are available for historians studying the period. It is certainly worth giving pupils examples of surviving sources – both written and visual – and asking them to comment on the sources' potential usefulness and reliability.

The Norman invasion

This is a splendid topic and worth spending some time on – although it is possible that some pupils will be full of it as a result of having covered it as part of the KS2 'Invaders and Settlers' unit. There are a host of possible activities. Pupils, for example, might be divided into five Witan groups. It is January 1066 and the groups have to decide who will be the next English king. Five individuals play the role of the claimants: Harold Godwinson, Harald Hadrada, Tostig, Edgar Atheling and Duke William of Normandy. They need to be articulate and reasonably well briefed. They rotate around the various groups, answering questions and presenting their case. A 'Question Time' format works just as well. Groups or individuals might follow up this activity by designing posters or writing political speeches for Harold, Harald, Tostig, Edgar and William.

Work on the Bayeux Tapestry might follow. For example give pupils mixed-up pictures and mixed-up captions of the Tapestry and get them to sequence the pictures as well as putting the right caption to the right picture. Pupils might also be asked to describe what they see in a particular picture (or pictures) and read out their answers to the class. Have all the pupils commented on the same things? Have some seen things which others have missed? Do they agree on what is happening in a particular picture?

Pupils might then design their own Bayeux Tapestry to show Harold's actions in September 1066. Individuals/pairs/groups could be given particular events to concentrate on, for example:

- Harold disbands his army
- Harald Hadrada sets sail from Norway
- Tostig joins Harald
- The Vikings (and Tostig) ravage the north-east coast of England
- The Vikings sail up the Humber
- Hadrada defeats earls Morcar and Edwin at Fulford

- The Vikings occupy York
- Harold marches north
- He sets out at dawn from Tadcaster
- A single Viking holds the bridge at Stamford Bridge
- Battle scenes of Stamford Bridge
- Harald Hadrada and Tostig are killed
- Only a few Viking ships sail home
- Harold celebrates his victory
- Harold hears news of the Norman invasion
- Harold's army sets off south

A good group work task is to discuss whether Harold should march from London to fight William in October 1066. What advice would the groups give Harold and why?

The Battle of Hastings is a good story in its own right. (The poem, 'I'll tell of the Battle of Hastings/As 'appened in days long gone by.' is worth reading). Follow-up work might include any of the following tasks:

- Pupils produce a newspaper front page or a radio/TV news report describing the Battle of Hastings.
- They write letters from a Norman knight or a surviving Saxon housecarl describing what happened at Hastings.
- Pupils write an appropriate piece for the Anglo-Saxon Chronicle describing the battle.
- They write William's official despatch telling the people of Normandy about the battle.

What happened to Harold is a good investigative mystery. Give the pupils the four or five 'primary' sources, especially the controversial scene from the Bayeux Tapestry, which provide some information about Harold's death. They must decide from the evidence what they think happened to Harold at Hastings. They can also be given such secondary opinions as the views of Sir Frank Stenton and Michael Wood.

The Norman impact

The main difficulty with this topic is that it is potentially very large, encompassing William's problems and actions immediately after Hastings, English resistance, motte and bailey castles, the feudal system and Domesday Book – all this to be fitted into one or at most two weeks.

Teachers are unlikely to focus on all these topics in the same depth. We would tend to concentrate on the way that William established control in England post-1066 and pay relatively little attention to the fine detail of the feudal system, accepting that some understanding of it is essential if pupils are to have any comprehension of medieval kingship and society. The following are possible teaching approaches:

- Pupils design a post-Battle of Hastings Bayeux Tapestry. What things would it have shown?

- Groups decide what William should do after Hastings (for example, return to Normandy, make friends with English nobles, reward followers with land, build good defences, punish the English who fought against him).

- Half the class writes an entry for the Anglo-Saxon Chronicle recording William's harrying of the North. The other half writes a Norman account. How do the accounts differ?

- Pupils design a 'wanted' poster for Hereward the Wake.

- They discuss William's need to establish strong points – and quickly. What type of 'castle' might William build and why?

- Give pupils evidence relating to the design of motte and bailey castles – for example, extracts from the Bayeux Tapestry showing Dinan castle, a contemporary account of the building of a Norman castle, post hole archaeological evidence, and an aerial photograph of a surviving motte. They are told to use the sources and their imagination to draw a reconstruction of a motte and bailey castle. They then have to label their diagrams to show the 'facts' – i.e. the information based on sources.

- They draw – or complete – a diagram to show how the feudal system worked. (They've being doing this for years and we can't think of a good reason why they should not continue to do so.)

- Pupils write an imaginary interview with a peasant in 1086. What might the peasant have said about the changes in his/her village over the past 20 years?

- They suppose that they are compiling a Domesday Book today. What questions would they ask?

- Give the pupils translated extracts from the Domesday Book. They have to work out what set of questions the real Domesday Book surveyors had to ask.

- Pupils write an obituary of William in 1087, or they suppose that they are a Norman knight, the wife of a Saxon lord, or a Saxon peasant and have been asked to comment on William's death. What might these different people have said?

Castles

The difficulty with this topic is controlling it. It is a full topic in its own right and is easier to teach over a term than over one or two weeks. There are no easy ways round this problem. If a lot of time is given to castles, something else has to give and there are so many potentially good topics in the 'Medieval Realms' unit that it is hard to know what should give. Moreover, it is difficult to see how this topic can be well taught unless pupils:

- have plenty of illustrative material
- work on an IT program
- watch a video on castles
- visit a local castle

But saying this simply makes the time problem worse. A visit (with preparation and debriefing) takes up at least one week's lesson time. IT programs, for example *Castle Life* and *Castle under Attack*, are similarly time-consuming. We have no real solutions to this problem. There are none – except to increase the amount of time made available for history.

We would, however, recommend that the topic is confined to castles in the late 11th and early 12th centuries. Motte and bailey castles can be dealt with when examining the Norman impact after 1066. Welsh castles can be examined when looking at Edward I's conquest of Wales. Learners can profitably do projects on castle development in the 14th and 15th centuries. 11th and 12th century castle activities could include:

- Groups discuss which of the following would be essential considerations when deciding where to build a stone castle:
    - Availability of materials
    - Availability of labour
    - Access to main routes
    - Ease of reaching all the main villages in the local area
    - Access to water
    - A natural strong point
    - Command of routeways

They go on to select the best site of a castle on the Welsh borders.

- Pupils design their own stone castle, labelling its main features.
- They plan an attack on a square keep castle.
- They write an estate agent's description of a square keep castle.
- They sequence jumbled pictures of castles, describing the main features of each castle in the process.

The medieval village

Pupils do not necessarily need to know a lot about the feudal system to appreciate this topic but it can help. The key question is, what was life like for most people in medieval England? The visual dimension, as always, is vital.

The following are possible activities:

- Give pupils an artist's impression/map of a medieval village (with numbered houses) and some descriptions/impressions of a variety of medieval people, for example priest, reeve, cottar, lord of the manor, bailiff, villein, blacksmith. The pupils have to match up the people and their (likely) homes.
- Learners describe a putative day trip to a medieval village, describing the people they met and what they did. What are the main differences between life then and now?
- They are given a list of farming activities. They have to decide which activity was likely to have been done in a particular season. (Some of the activities might have been done throughout the year.) Activities might include things like finding firewood, repairing houses, making tools, threshing, winnowing, slaughtering, lambing, building, milking, ploughing, collecting, bird scaring, muck spreading, harvesting, etc.
- They design an estate agent's description of a villein's home.
- Groups discuss which of the following a medieval woman would have found most useful:
  - One year's supply of rushes for the floor
  - One year's free rent
  - 100 litres of milk
  - A well outside her cottage
  - A bigger and faster spinning machine
  - Ten kilos of oats
  - A new cow
  - A horse
  - A nanny for her three children
  - A large feast with as much food as she could eat for a week
  - A servant
  - More land

They can select three things and have to say why they have chosen these items. They should bear in mind that there was no electricity, no fridges and no piped water in medieval times (and servants needed feeding).

The medieval town

The emphasis is likely to be on what life was like in medieval towns and how these towns were different from towns today. There are several towns which have preserved something of their medieval past – if only their walls – and which are thus worth a visit. York is our favourite. It has walls, Clifford's tower (with another motte just across the river), the Shambles,

the Minster, the Merchant Adventurers' Hall, the Houlgate 'Viking' centre
– which can easily be regarded as medieval – and the Yorkshire Museum.
Classroom activities could include:

● Give pupils a map showing possible sites for a new town – for example,
  near a castle, near a monastery, on a river, on a road, near to several villages, near to water, at a cross roads, etc. Individually or in groups, they
  must select the best site.
● Learners label a printed diagram of a typical medieval town.
● They suppose that they are modern day health inspectors. They produce
  a report on the hazards of life in a typical medieval town.
● Divide the class into several guilds, representing different 'trades'.
  Each guild has to design its own banner, draw up a list of five rules
  which members of the guild must obey and decide what punishments to
  mete out to people who disobey the rules.

Medieval law and order

This is not a particularly important topic but because it is gory it tends to
capture learners' imaginations. A good activity is to divide them into
groups, representing aldermen judging certain criminals. Provide the
groups with lists of criminals and crimes. Also give the groups lists of possible medieval punishments. (Jordan and Wood provide such lists in *England in the Middle Ages*.) The groups must choose a punishment to fit the
crime and also be ready to justify their decision. Each group member
should then produce an illustrated account explaining the crimes they
tried, the punishments they gave and why they made their decisions.

Discussion of law and order in medieval times can easily lead into a
good discussion of crime and punishment today. Do severe punishments
deter?

The medieval church

The role of the church in medieval society is an important but not necessarily an intrinsically interesting topic. A visit to a local medieval church
or cathedral, perhaps in conjunction with the RE department, might be a
way of introducing or completing it.

Classroom activities might include:

● Pupils draw a diagram to show how the church (as a whole) was organised.
● Groups try and work out their responses to the following:

  – Why was the church so important in the Middle Ages?
  – What kinds of things might parish priests do?

– What kinds of things might rich and poor people do to avoid going to hell? (for example, go on Crusade, go on a pilgrimage, give money to do good things, give money for prayers to be said for them after they died, give money to build churches). Which do they think was the best bet?

● Pupils write an advertisement for the post of a parish priest, explaining what sort of person should apply for the job and what he will be expected to do.

Monasteries and nunneries

The main emphasis here is likely to be on what life was like in a medieval monastery or nunnery. A visit to the ruins of a monastery or nunnery is a 'must' if there is one in your locality. Teachers might get pupils to do one or more of the following tasks in the classroom:

● Devise their own monastic rules, saying what monks or nuns should do at each hour of the day. They then compare this with the rule of St Benedict.
● Write, tape-record or draw strip pictures of a typical day in the life of a monk or nun.
● Pupils are given details of a typical day of a monk or nun. They have to produce a graph showing how long monks and nuns spent on each of the following activities:
  – church services
  – work
  – sleep
  – meals
  – private reading or praying
  – leisure time

● Give learners a list of possible monkish activities. They have to arrange the activities into two columns headed: Likely activities for monks; Unlikely activities for monks. Activities might include praying, gardening, bee-keeping, copying books, gambling, learning to fight, brewing ale, fishing, fasting, singing, weaving, mixing medicine, baking, riding, begging, shopping, looking after guests, painting, building, carpentry, dancing. They choose two activities from the unlikely column and explain why they put them there.
● They discuss how we know what a typical monk's day was like. Was there ever such a thing? Is there such a thing as a typical pupil's day at school?
● They plan a new monastery or nunnery. (They already have some idea

of the types of rooms they must include in their building.)

● Monks/nuns do not seem to have had a very enjoyable life – so get pupils to discuss why a person became a monk/nun.

The death of Thomas Becket

This topic provides an excellent story. It also has considerable potential for source-based investigative work. Most National Curriculum textbooks contain a reasonable selection of sources which provide information about the circumstances surrounding Becket's death (for example, Edward Grim's account, William fitzStephen's account, near contemporary illustrations, etc.). Pupils might play the part of 'detectives', working out the bias and reliability of the sources, and deciding who was responsible for Becket's death.

Another possibility is for groups of pupils to record a TV news report of Becket's death. All the members of the group have to be involved in the performance. There can be two newsreaders, religious and political correspondents, and others can play the part of eye-witnesses who are being interviewed.

The Crusades

This is a colossal topic and one which some schools will have taught as a unit in its own right. Those schools will probably continue to cover the topic in some depth. Our inclination would be to cover the topic superficially. We would get the pupils to consider the causes of the Crusades, perhaps getting them to write a speech for Pope Urban designed to persuade people to go on Crusade. Or we might get groups discussing why people went on Crusade, hoping to make the point that Crusaders had a variety of motives.

A timeline of the main events of the Crusades – with pupils designing a few small illustrations to accompany the events – would take us through to discussion of the main short and long term results of the Crusades. Pupils might do a project on an aspect of Crusading warfare in our final unit on medieval warfare.

Robin Hood – did he exist?

We like this topic – and so do pupils. It is not simply light relief but gets pupils straight into the important issue of popular myth and can also help them to an understanding of the problems of sources. It is, too, a good opportunity to examine the way that Robin Hood has been portrayed on film this century. There is a wealth of potential film material, for example:

Robin of Sherwood (an ITV series), *The Adventures of Robin Hood* (1938), *Robin and Marion* (1976) and *Robin Hood: Prince of Thieves* (1992). Pupils might be asked to comment on which gives the most accurate picture of life in medieval England in the late 12th century. It is also possible to have a class debate on whether Robin Hood existed or not.

Medieval kingship

Most pupils are more interested in real individuals whom they get to know than in medieval monarchy as a concept. So we recommend that you concentrate on one or two medieval monarchs. A case can be made for almost any of them. William Rufus died a good (i.e. mysterious) death. Henry I's reign involved the incident of the White Ship. Stephen's reign was a time of brutality. Henry II's reign was long and significant (the film *The Lion in Winter* might be a useful resource). The study of Richard I gets you immediately into the Crusades – and so it goes on.

We would recommend examining the reign of King John. The obvious link with Robin Hood is worth making because it opens up the question of whether King John was really such a villain, although if there was a Robin Hood he lived neither in Richard's reign, nor in John's. The reign also involves a host of important issues – not least the struggle with church and barons which culminated with Magna Carta. There is also something to be said for looking at Henry III's reign as a follow up to John and, in particular, the King's struggle with Simon de Montfort.

Activities might include:

- Pupils design a timeline of the English kings from William I to Henry V.
- They design a Magna Carta – for display purposes. The document should look genuine with sealing wax, etc.
- They do a 'This is Your Life' script for whichever king they have studied in depth.

Ireland, Wales and Scotland

Teaching pupils about England's relations with Ireland, Wales and Scotland is a real challenge. It involves a lot of difficult concepts and a need for a real awareness of maps and geography. There is the constant danger of getting bogged down in detail. If you take this topic seriously, we suggest concentrating on one of the countries and covering the other two superficially. Take your pick. A good case can be made for each of them.

Ireland

● Pupils might plan an interview with a variety of English and Irish nobles in the 12th century. What questions might have been asked? What might have been the response?

● Pupils write an obituary of Strongbow, Earl of Pembroke.

Wales

● Groups might play the part of advisors to Edward I. How would they suggest he goes about conquering Wales?

● Pupils imagine they are Welsh scouts sent to spy on the newly built Harlech (Caernarvon, Beaumaris, Conway) castle. Provide them with pictures and plans of the castle. They have to make a report of what they have seen to Welshmen who are considering fighting against the English. Would they advise attacking Harlech? If they do advise an attack, how might it be launched?

Scotland

● Pupils might design a wanted poster for either William Wallace or Robert Bruce.

● They might design a poster intended to persuade Scots to fight against the English.

● Half the class writes a Scottish front page of a newspaper to celebrate the battle of Bannockburn: the other half writes the front page of an English newspaper. How are the two reports different?

● Get them to write an imaginary interview with Robert Bruce in 1326. What questions might Bruce have been asked? What might he have replied?

Medicine

This is easy. We recommend you buy and play Jordan and Wood's medieval medicine game, described in Chapter 3.

The Black Death

This is another popular topic. We think the emphasis should be on how it arrived and what effect it had, both immediately and in the medium and long term. The following are possible activities:

● Give groups of pupils a collection of primary and secondary sources. They must use the sources to decide how the Black Death came to England, what caused it, and what effect it had on those who caught it. The groups report their conclusions to the other groups.

- Make the point to pupils that people in the 14th century did not know what caused the Black Death but they had several views. Give individuals or groups some beliefs about how to avoid the Plague including:
    - Avoid breathing in germs when with a plague victim;
    - Sit next to a blazing fire, as the Pope did, right through the hot summer of 1348;
    - Attack foreigners and Jews;
    - Live in a house sheltered from the wind and keep the windows closed;
    - Buy a lucky charm;
    - Travel about in groups whipping each other as punishment for sins;
    - Pray.

Which of these strategies might have been some use – and which of no use – in helping to avoid catching the plague? If pupils had been alive in the 14th century, which view might have impressed them?

- Jordan and Wood have devised an interesting History Action Pack simulation entitled *The Black Death*. This can work well but requires several sharp, confident and articulate pupils to role play certain characters if it is to be really successful.
- Pupils write a diary that someone might have kept during the plague year. They make entries before the plague began, while it was going on, and after it ended.
- They suppose that they are a reeve in 1349. They must prepare a report for their lord outlining the problems faced in their village, especially noting which jobs it will be difficult to get done.
- Groups discuss the likely results of the Black Death. What do they think might have been the most important result?

The Peasants' Revolt

This is another popular topic and one well covered in most of the National Curriculum textbooks. It is a good story, there are excellent source-based possibilities and it's a good topic for getting learners to consider what they might have done as leaders of the peasants or as the King at various times during the crisis.

Possible activities include:

- Pupils draw a comic strip of the main events of the Peasants Revolt.
- Give the pupils a list of jumbled events of the Peasants Revolt. They have to put them in sequence.
- Pupils imagine they are peasant leaders. They write a letter to Richard II

setting out their grievances.

- Groups make a TV news report of the main events, interviewing some of the main leaders of both sides.
- Groups decide what advice they would have given to Wat Tyler at Blackheath in 1381. They explain their advice to the other groups. Then they go on to decide what advice they would have given King Richard II in 1381. Again they explain their advice to the other groups.
- Give the pupils a variety of sources to enable them to consider the events at Smithfield. They then have to write a biased radio/TV news account, supporting the King's side or the peasants. It is possible to set up a 'real' newsroom situation and feed them bits of information at a time, for example, weather forecast, events abroad, events elsewhere in Britain and Europe.
- Pupils design a wanted poster for John Ball.
- Pupils write an obituary for Wat Tyler.

Medieval warfare

This is a useful 'catch-all' topic and we suggest that individuals or groups could produce a project on one of the following topics:

- Crusading warfare
- A study of one of the Crusades
- 14th and 15th century castles
- Becoming a knight
- Armour (there may be an opportunity for a local brass rubbing)
- Tournaments
- Any battle from the Hundred Years War (for example, Crecy, Agincourt)
- Joan of Arc
- Any battle from the Wars of the Roses (especially if there is a local one)
- Warwick the Kingmaker
- Lady Margaret Beaufort
- Heraldry
- Richard III
- The Battle of Bosworth

Pupils have to tell – or show – the rest of the class what they have done.

Medieval Realms – conclusion

It is important to end any topic with some kind of pulling together or debriefing session. Groups of pupils, for example, might decide what things had changed and what things had stayed much the same between

1066 and 1500. They might discuss what events they regard as the most important in the period. They might evaluate the unit as a whole and discuss which topic they have most enjoyed and why.

The making of the United Kingdom – crowns, parliaments and peoples 1500–1750

Overview

In many ways this is a comfortable old standby of secondary school history and in its current incarnation represents a welcome slimming-down of the 1990 National Curriculum. Yet what is left is not entirely comfortable. Three requirements that cause concern are:

● The need to cover Ireland, Wales, Scotland and England. It is hard to believe that this can be taken seriously. Not only are three of these areas poorly covered in the available resources, but it is hard to arouse much interest (except amongst Cromwell-worshippers) for the 1536 Act of Union.
● Other political topics verge upon the unteachable (the Glorious Revolution) or are usually managed only by trivialisation and distortion (the Reformation, the English Civil War).
● No-one can take the 1750 finishing date seriously, unless they propose to examine politics as analysed by J.C.D. Clarke. In practice 1689 will be the finishing point. Going into the 18th Century is entering a quagmire as far as political history is concerned and trespassing on material usually handled within Core Unit 3. It is somewhat redeemed by the idea of telling children that there was a War of Jenkins' Ear and by looking at the vivid topic of the Fifteen and the Forty-five.

We shall now discuss approaches to the main stream of this unit. First, we need to insist that it is still not a comfortable topic to teach. Particular problems are:

● the prominence of detail in complex political themes;
● bitter arguments over religious ideology and complex constitutional positions (*pace* the 'revisionists'), which can seem sterile and stupid;
● the complexity of the sources compared to those for the Middle Ages, exacerbated by the fact that since they are written in English, there is a temptation to present them directly to learners;
● given that in many areas of the UK the surviving sources do not allow for much independent, discovery learning, the unit will tend to be heavily teacher-organised;

- the amount that might be covered – this is a large topic.

This unit has a lot of scope for the development of cross-curricular themes. The theme of citizenship is obvious and can be well organised around the moral issue of human rights. Environmental issues can be raised in the context of the impact of population and urban growth and of new agricultural and industrial methods upon the environment. These developments also raise questions about healthy living, although most learners will not immediately see a connection between the unhealthy towns of Stuart England and deprived areas of some modern British cities.

Three other points about this unit are:

- There is relatively little argument about *what* happened, but there is much rancour about causes, outcomes and the significance of people and of events. We suggest that the concept of historical interpretation should pervade this topic.
- Politically, there is no denying the change from medieval monarchy to oligarchic monarchy, although explanations for this are plentiful and complex. Some modern historians have emphasised the fragility of Parliament's position, even in the early 18th century. We echo that.
- Economically and socially Britain changed between 1500 and 1700 (rather as it did between 1100 and 1300). Changes may be noticed but without denying the forces of inertia, such that the fundamental pre-industrial lifestyle was changed only at the edges.

Introducing the era

Nowadays, learners should come to this unit with a good grasp of two things which formerly could not be taken for granted:

1. They should have some notion of when the year 1500 is in relation to previous times and to now.
2. They should have a notion of what England in 1500 was like and how it differed from England in, say, 1066.

It may still be wise to begin the unit with an activity intended to consolidate this introductory awareness. For example, using work on medieval England and collections of mainly pictorial resources showing early Tudor life, pupils could be arranged into different groups, each with a brief to describe key features of different Tudor lives (rich/poor, town/country, men's/women's). This is essentially a research exercise. Results could be presented in a prepared grid or through a series of displays, annotated posters, brief oral presentations or short, acted sketches showing typical themes.

A sharp slide-show can then reinforce learners' images of the 'tudorness' of Tudor times, as can skilled use of video clips, posters or postcards.

Work should also be done to check what learners already know about this period and to probe their grasp of key concepts such as 'church', 'parliament', 'Civil War', 'economy', and 'social'. It is best if a history department draws upon the wisdom of its members to make up a quiz that tests learners' grasp of what it regards as key knowledge and conceptual understanding. The results of this quiz, which can be done in a fairly light-hearted way, should inform the way the topic is produced.

The Reformation

By any standards, this is an unfriendly topic with which to begin a unit. It compounds difficulties to give it the attention that it gets in most textbooks, especially as they generally swallow the orthodoxies that the Catholic church was a mess on the eve of the Reformation; that England settled to a new religion; and that the Dissolution of the Monasteries was a disaster for the poor.

We suggest taking this topic briskly. Learners would be introduced to the bones of the topic, which would be consolidated by some material to read. Two questions could organise the activities:

- Is there any reason to be suspicious of sources, such as the work of Simon Fish, saying that the Catholic church was corrupt on the eve of the Reformation?
- What did the Reformation change?

Activities could include:

- Comparison of sources saying that the Church was corrupt in 1529 with some of the many 'puritan' tracts saying the same in the 1570s.
- A mix and match exercise called 'in whose interests..?' A variety of claims about the Catholic church to be matched with the names of people or groups who had an interest in making those claims.
- Using a teacher-assembled bank of edited sources, including ones showing the limits to Protestant impact as late as the 1570s, draw up a balance sheet of change and continuity. A refinement is to ask about change and continuity from different points of view – how would the Reformation have seemed to villagers in NW England? To London craftsmen?
- Making a 'before and after' poster or writing a newspaper article as if it were a 1547 review of what Henry had achieved in religion.

It's impossible to leave Henry VIII out of this unit. We suggest *telling* Henry's story, making it a human story of a golden youth's attempt to please himself and to settle the future of his country: a tragedy – and for his wives too. This might be followed up by groups preparing to interview Henry, drawing up lists of, say, ten key questions to ask him. If there is time, some might interview the teacher in role. If there is more time, some of the learners might try and take on Henry's role, which should lead to lively discussion between 'Henry' and his interviewers.

The reign of Elizabeth

Traditionally, there are four foci to this attractive topic: Parliament, Religion, foreign affairs and Gloriana. We suggest cutting it to three, leaving out Parliament. The importance of the disputes – if they can be called that – between Elizabeth and her parliaments has been exaggerated, and the power of the House of Commons has been misrepresented. In contrast, the influence of the court, nobility and Council has been underplayed, and the Elizabethan Age has been depicted as a proto-constitutional monarchy, rather than as the medieval monarchy that it more closely resembled.

Religion

Religion might be tackled as a decision-making exercise. Present the situation as it was in 1558, with a Catholic country, a Protestant, moderate queen and some more extreme Protestant voices. Consider the deficiencies of the church – ignorance, poverty, pluralism and corruption. This might be based upon a teacher-produced collection of sources.

Before going any further it is necessary to ask, why should anyone treat religion as a problem? Why did differences in religious beliefs matter? If learners do not see that it was thought a country could not survive if it contained two religions; that toleration was not seen as a virtue but as a sin, since that meant allowing people to go to Hell for having heretical beliefs; and that religion permeated life, this theme will make little sense. So, what should Elizabeth do? Learners might draw up a six-point, 15 year plan, adding a sentence to each point to say what would have to be done to bring about each action point.

Comparison with what happened should follow, leading to questions about the wisdom of Elizabeth's actions, which will be all the sharper since the class has already said what it would have done. Why did Elizabeth act as she did? At this point it would be useful to jump to 1603 and summarise the religious situation, showing how England was essentially a Protestant country by then, although complaints continued, as James I was to find out.

A forceful way of concluding this exercise is to have learners draw up two columns, one listing Elizabethan religious successes, the other listing things still to be done. With luck, the second column will contain more points than the first. The value comes from probing the assumption that Elizabeth's work had failed because the areas in need of attention outnumbered the areas of success.

Foreign affairs

An outline map should be shaded to show England's actual and potential enemies in 1558. A note should be added to explain why each foe was hostile – or potentially hostile – to England.

Again, a prediction exercise gives an edge to what is to come. As an observer in 1558, what future would you have predicted for England? What strategies might enable England to survive as an independent nation? Were there any advantages that England had in this desperate struggle for independence? Notice that while this work depends on learners receiving a lot of information from teachers or books, they are required to make active use of it.

Following our inclination for stories, we would then use the story of Mary, Queen of Scots to carry the matter of Anglo-French relations. A good starting point is her execution. Then organise the story around the question of whether she was unlucky or foolish. This can be sharpened by stopping the tale at key points and doing one or two things. One is to ask learners to predict what would happen next, while the other is to ask them to think about the most recent segment of the tale and decide whether it shows Mary as a victim or a poor judge of people and circumstances. While this might be presented as an essay, an interview or a 'Mills and Boon' story, a lot of pointless writing can be cut out by asking learners to annotate scenes from Mary's life (which might be legitimately photocopied from various older school texts), or to produce a six-frame cartoon showing turning points in her life.

The story of the Spanish Armada is another good one to tell, stopping if you wish at key points for discussion. The main activity will be to ask why the Armada failed. This can be done in a number of ways – pupils are given a list of possible causes, such as Medina del Sidonia's leadership, asked to write a sentence of explanation against each and then to rank the causes in order of importance; pupils produce a Spanish and an English newspaper account of the débâcle; they prepare and conduct interviews with people in role as key players in the Armada, such as Effingham, Queen Elizabeth, Parma and Philip II. In addition, this theme is quite well served by collections of primary sources and there is room to investigate discrepancies, as well as to extend or replace the teacher-led story with accounts drawn up by learners using these sources.

As a matter of historical completeness, it is worth noticing that the demise of the Armada was not the end of the story – it was not until the

17th century that the costly war with Spain was concluded. We will barely notice the great theme of seadogs and colonists, which takes us well into the Stuart era, since time may be too tight for it to be more than mentioned. When working on the Tudor privateers, we want to raise questions about the difference between terrorist and patriot, pirate and hero. The colonisation of the New World is organised partly around the motives people had for going, including the power of myth, but it is dominated by the interaction of different races: by questions about civilised society, about cultural differences and about morality.

Gloriana

What is the official image of Elizabeth and of her court? There are plenty of activities that can be centred on the reading of visual propaganda to understand how Elizabeth wished to be seen – as Gloriana. Sellar and Yeatman's verdict that Elizabeth was 'in every respect a good and romantic queen' should not lightly be discarded but there is another view, and learners should encounter criticisms of timidity, of meanness, of the long, wearing Spanish war, of court corruption and high taxation, and of the persecution of the more zealous Protestants (who were often nicknamed 'puritans'). It is quite likely that the achievements will be rated more highly than the criticisms but it would be possible to attribute them to luck rather than judgement, so that the Queen could be called 'Elizabeth the Lucky' rather than 'Gloriana'. Techniques for presenting this work include: doing a balance sheet of achievements and failings; writing an obituary for Elizabeth; making up an Elizabethan album of pictures of high points and low points; discussions, debates and mock interviews with pupils in role as various Elizabethan people.

Living in Tudor times

Judgement of Elizabeth's reign needs to be set against an understanding of the social and economic conditions of the times, and might be best delayed until this section of work has been done. Bear in mind that learners are likely to retain some grasp of this topic from their KS2 work.

In many ways this is the largest and most powerful element of this core unit. Suggestions include:

● Take the ideas suggested for the medieval village, town and law and order and apply them to Tudor times. There's a good case for saying that little had changed.

● What sources might tell us about how people lived in Elizabethan times? What are their strengths (for example, parish registers are often printed in English and held in public libraries) and weaknesses (often there are sharp limits to what you can learn from parish registers)? Which sources are available locally? This might lead to the production of a brief guide, *Finding out about Tudor times in Ourtown*.

- Use the computer to analyse parish register data (a sample of which ought long ago to have been stored on a suitable database), raising questions such as 'at what age did males/females die?', 'how many children did women have?', 'did more people die at some times of the year than at others?' (And what hypotheses can learners offer for the pattern they will find?) Many registers will allow much more complex enquiries than these, but some are minimalist.

- Produce a guide to a Tudor site or building. This is a more powerful activity if the guide is written from a particular perspective, as if a servant or rich lady or visitor from the countryside were the guide. As a result, we'd not be told that 'these are the kitchens', but 'this is where I work...it's hot by the fire but...' or 'this is where the servants prepare our food. They have to...' or 'kitchens, they call them! It's bigger than my cottage'. Texts, videos, slides and reference books can be used to help learners provide authentic illustrations.

- Take a theme – diet, dress, education, medicine and health, for example – and approach it with respect to two different groups of Tudor people. The task is not simply to work on primary and secondary sources to build up a picture of this theme in respect to those two perspectives, but also to ask deeper questions – especially 'why did they do/believe this?' and 'was there anything that they could have done, in the circumstances, to improve it?'

- Take an activity – cooking, arable farming, shipbuilding, for example. Split a page into three columns. The thin, left hand column names the main stages of the activity and might refer the reader to accompanying photocopies. The second and widest column explains what is involved in this stage. The last column tries to say why they did it in this way.

- Take a clip from a schools video programme and turn down the sound. Get groups of learners to supply commentary, if need be freeze-framing at points of particular interest.

- Produce annotated displays showing aspects of Tudor life 'with attitude' – that is, the commentary should reflect a stance and go beyond description.

- Go into drama. Produce – or have pupils produce – 'role cards' which describe a role in a village (farrier, gentlewoman, goodwife, cottager) or in a town (preacher, beggar). Give each player a role card and make time for them to do research into the role. If there is more than one person with the same role, they might want to work together on this and to think together about what their role involves. In addition, some of the characters get 'action cards', describing something that they have to do.

After the research, set people working together in role. Be prepared to stop the action by 'freeze-framing' it and invite the audience to question individual actors about what they are doing, why they are doing it and how they feel about their work, life and surroundings.

While there is value in this, greater learning can take place if new elements are injected into the scene – a proclamation is read out saying that taxes have to be raised for the Spanish wars, or there is news that the plague has reached neighbouring villages, or actors are told that bad weather means the harvest will be inadequate. The actors have to respond to these announcements, working out ways of coping with them.

At these points it can be useful for the teacher to go into role as some kind of expert – a wizard or wise woman, a village elder or the JP – and to be available for questioning by the actors as a way of opening up to them possibilities for consideration.

This needs to be spread over several lessons, with action leading to opportunities for further research and preparation: an interplay of historical research and of the 'empathy' that comes from problem-working in role. For many of us the big problem would be finding enough time for this active approach.

- A follow-up activity involves learners interviewing each other in pairs, where one of them is 'in role'.
- Comparison is a powerful tool for active thinking. Ask learners to compare the medieval town or village with its Tudor equivalent; with villages they have studied in other places and times; or with the present. What are the sources of the differences and of the similarities?
- Invent a village or a family and try to reconstruct it as authentically as possible. This can be done as a group, individual or whole-class activity.
- Priorities. Ask learners to list, say, ten things that they would have liked about living in a certain role in a specified Tudor setting. Had they lived in that role, what things might they have feared? What might they have hoped for?
- Ask pupils what things we don't seem to know about Tudor life, which will point them towards the voices that have not survived, especially those of poor women, and to our relative ignorance about the taken-for-granted and about feelings. What sort of evidence would tell us about these neglected themes? Why don't we have it? What prospects are there that we might learn more about them?

James I

Academic thinking about the reign of James I has been substantially revised over the past twenty years, although not all school books reflect this. It is possible to plough through James' financial problems (exaggerated?), problems with parliaments (exaggerated), eirenic foreign policy, and relations with the puritans (whoever they were), but we suggest concentrating on two issues.

1. Verdicts on James – many accounts of him repeat the virulent attack made by the disappointed courtier Sir Anthony Weldon. This can be found in S. J. Houston's *James I* (Longman, 1973). You may wish to edit it first. One way of working on it is to ask pupils to identify the different criticisms Weldon made and against each suggest something that would support the claim. So, James is accused of cowardice and learners are asked what would count as evidence of his cowardice. A taxing activity is for them to then search available materials to see what evidence they can find to support Weldon's claims. Alternatively, present them with other views (also in Houston's book) and ask learners to adjudicate, making it clear where the answer ought to be one of uncertainty.

2. The Gunpowder Plot – this is too well-known and too well-resourced a tale not to be covered. It is worth telling a Gunpowder Plot story and then saying that this is a version based upon the evidence, before turning to the sources as a detective work activity, designed to see how close we can get to solving the mystery of who tipped off Lord Mounteagle.

The outbreak of war

By now it is no longer possible to ignore parliaments, which we have cheerfully done hitherto. Yet it is equally hard to know how to treat them, especially as scholarship over the past 20 years has called into question many assumptions about the growth of parliamentary power. We suggest that the focus be on the years 1640–2. Background will have to be filled in, notably:

● What was a parliament? What was it for? What did it do? The trick here is to avoid suggesting that Stuart parliaments were more awkward than their Tudor or medieval forebears.
● The eleven year personal rule. Again there is a problem, since we hear the version told by the victors of the 1640s and far less of the evidence that this was not a doomed, nor a particularly tyrannical enterprise.

This might be done around an exposition of Charles's dilemma – how was he to run and reform a country when parliaments, the traditional way of offering advice and (financial) support had become so constipated?

Likewise, it is hard to see alternatives to a heavily edited account of the years 1640–2, stressing that:

- war was not inevitable;
- all parties proclaimed their loyalty to the King;
- events in Scotland and Ireland produced an impossible emergency for the crown;
- Charles's strategies could be questioned.

We know that this sorry story can be supported with many primary sources, although it is arguable whether they clarify or confuse. Although the usual devices can be used to involve learners in this narrative – stopping the story for discussion, for research, and for learners to say what they think would happen next – they have hitherto been essentially passive. If they are helped to identify a set of causes of the Civil War, they can be more involved through two sets of activities:

1. Sorting causes into sets, particularly into 'long-term' and 'short-term' causes. A number will fall between the two sets and should stay there.
2. Identifying the most important cause or small group of causes of the War. Many of the sorting and ranking methods described in the last chapter are appropriate.

A useful way of summarising this story is to cast it into the form of a flowchart or render it as a set of cartoons.

The English Civil War, Protectorate and Restoration

It's possible to teach the battles of the Civil War, but we don't. The chaotic, balkanised divisions of the years 1642–9 we also avoid.

What's left? Charles was executed when it became increasingly clear that while he lived no settlement would stay settled for long and Cromwell came to dominate the Republic. It is possible to look at the treatment of Royalists, at 'puritan' reforms and at the way monarchical forms re-emerged, but it is hard to work up conviction about governments which even their supporters saw as failures. The Republic's undoubted military triumphs and the blot of Drogheda could be covered, but they look odd if they dominate work on the period between 1642 and 1660.

In short, these are exceptionally difficult years to handle at any level and unless you want to take a biographical approach to Cromwell, probably organised around the dilemma of whether he was an honest man 'waiting on the Lord' or a hypocrite who 'will weep, howl and repent even while he doth smite you under the first rib', it is hard to get a grip on them.

Our preference is evident. Go for the colourful events – the abolition of Christmas, battles, executions, and massacres, if you wish. We cover these years through a succinct narrative, as we do the Restoration.

Plague and Fire

These two events are here because they are spectacular and generally go down well.

For the plague, we adapt the Jordan and Wood medieval material, adding to it edited contemporary sources, such as extracts from Pepys' ubiquitous diary. Two questions organise activities on the Plague:

1. What happened? Learners construct accounts from collections of sources.
2. Why did people use the remedies they did and why weren't modern remedies used?

The second question is an important one for getting at the idea that people acted sensibly within the confines of their beliefs. Treat it in the ways that we recommended for the Black Death and medieval medicine.

This may be a good point to pick up the topic of witchcraft, although it belongs chronologically with James I rather than Charles II, who was not a witch burner. The idea of some people being able to tap supernatural powers for good purposes (priests, wise men and wise women) and for evil (witches and warlocks) goes well with the plague. Apart from the obvious possibilities for source-based work, this is a topic distinguished by its appeal to the imagination, not by opportunities for active history.

Much the same can be said for the Great Fire. Like the Plague, it can be organised around activities on the causes of the Fire, as they were seen at the time, and on attempts to fight it. The conventional wisdom that the subsequent rebuilding of London in stone helped to eradicate the Plague could be questioned vigorously – Dickens presents a picture of a Victorian London that would be ideal for another plague.

Revolution and wars

This area is widely neglected and since most schools will have little time for it we shall touch lightly upon it.

The causes of the 1688 Revolution can be treated in the same way as the causes of the Civil War. Particular attention should be directed towards the similarities and the differences between the two revolts. There is also scope for taking the Bill of Rights and asking learners to consider what difference it would have made to different groups of people – Catholic gentry, Protestant gentry, women and male cottagers, for example.

The Jacobites, the '15 and the '45 make for good stories in which different points of view can be explored, probably within the same framework as the story of English overseas colonisation.

1500–1700: continuity and change

To compare across two centuries, pupils will need a lot of evidence about the state of England in 1700. Much of this will be visual material, but statistics for trade and population can be used, along with probate inventories, maps and the whole range of written sources, including, perhaps, extracts from early 18th century novels.

Having formed a view of England *circa* 1700, comparison is possible. We suggest that class discussion is used to identify headings for comparison – trade, agriculture, industry, wealth – as well as perspectives for comparison – poor men, poor women, nobles and merchants, for example. The fundamental question, which can be worked through in many ways, was whether England in 1700 was more different from or more similar to England in 1500. It might be worth revisiting this question after work on core unit 3, which will allow comparison with late Victorian times. There would then be a place for a sketch graph showing the rate of change in the lives of different groups of people across the years 1100–1900. Of course, change is not to be confused with progress, and it may be felt that for some groups, some periods of change were change for the worse.

Endnote

If you want a really active way of teaching any of these topics, why not arrange for secondary pupils to 'teach' them to primary school children?

Britain 1750–c. 1900

Overview

This unit is similar, but not identical, to the old National Curriculum unit 'Expansion, trade and industry'. Pupils should be given an overview of major developments in the period and, in particular, of the impact on Britain of world-wide expansion, industrialisation and political developments. The focus should be on how these combined to shape nineteenth-century Britain. They should be taught about an aspect of the period in depth.

Pupils should be given an overview of the following:

- The growth of trade and Empire and its impact on Britain and the colonies;
- Industrial change and its impact on the way of life of people at different levels of society;
- The influence of personalities and events, including the American Revolution, the French Revolution and the Napoleonic Wars; popular protest and reform; and the extension of the franchise, including the Reform Act of 1832.

They should have opportunities to study in depth at least one related topic, for example, Britain and the American Revolution; the Napoleonic Wars and key personalities such as Nelson and Wellington; the slave trade and its abolition; the development of Empire in an area such as India or Africa; the role of an inventor, entrepreneur, explorer, individual reformer or politician; a political protest or reform movement such as Chartism; the role of a national political leader such as Pitt, Peel, Gladstone or Disraeli; relations between Ireland and Britain; the development of legislation to improve working and living conditions; the impact of the period on the development of the arts and architecture; and industrialisation in a local area.

The main difficulty is that there is still far too much content to cover. At first glance it appears as though the content has been cut. Industrialisation has replaced 'social and economic change in Britain' which included changes in agriculture, industry and transport; the impact of economic change on families and communities, working and living conditions, and the size and distribution of Britain's population; religious differences and links between religion and social reform. However, 'Industrialisation' is a broad term. Many will think it impossible to teach the industrial revolution without first doing something on the interesting themes of the agricultural and the transport revolutions. The topic suddenly begins to look fearsomely large again. The political developments have grown. The American and French Revolutions and the Napoleonic Wars now have to be taught. Teachers are also expected to study in depth at least one 'related' topic. There is a full year's work here – and only a term and a half to deliver.

Another difficulty is the fact that many schools offer British Social and Economic History at GCSE. These schools have to provide a coherent course both for those pupils who complete their study of history at the end of Y9 and those who continue until Y11. There is a real danger of replicating topics. Careful planning is essential to ensure that those who abandon history at 14 have some notion of the main events of the period but that there is not too much overlapping for those who continue at GCSE.

On the positive side there is considerable potential for local study work. Changes to the local area may not only be a useful starting point, but may well be the focus of the Industrialisation topic in particular. Information on the locality can be found out from old maps, paintings, engravings, street names, documents in local archive collections, census returns and from local histories. There are thousands of potential places to visit ranging from theme museums/sites (for example, Quarry Bank at Styal) to local transport, industrial, urban and agricultural sites. However, visits are time consuming and make the content overload situation that much worse.

Given the GCSE complication, the local dimension and the fact that the proposals give schools considerable freedom of choice in terms of selecting a study in depth, schemes of work will vary massively from school to school. In this situation, our intention is to indicate the topics which might be studied by pupils in Y9. But we know that many schools will find it impossible to cover some of the topics at all. Much of what we suggest applies both to Y9 groups and to groups studying British Social and Economic history for GCSE.

The key questions arising from this unit for Y9 pupils might be:

- Why and how did Britain become a great trading and imperial power in the period 1750–1900?
- What impact did the Industrial Revolution have on Britain?
- What were the main political developments in the period?

A key concept is likely to be the notion of revolution. Pupils are likely to encounter several, including the industrial, agricultural, transport, American, and French revolutions.

Introducing the unit

One way to introduce the unit is to get pupils to brainstorm what they know about the period as a whole. Another is to get pupils to consider and examine the types of sources which have survived and which are essential to studying the period. Again, give groups statistics of the British population in 1750 and 1900 and have groups decide why the growth of population might have occurred and what its results might have been. Schools which intend concentrating on the local area (and which have good maps and visual sources) could compare the area in 1750 with the area in 1900 (and with today).

The agricultural revolution

If learners are going to understand the impact of the industrial revolution on Britain and on the local area, they will need to know something of what it was like c.1750. Robert Unwin invariably makes use of an excellent engraving of a mid-18th century farming scene. Pupils are asked what they can see in the picture and in particular how many people are at work. What types of work are people doing? Why did 18th century farms employ so many people? We can think of few better starting points.

After this pupils might:

- In groups work out why they think there was a growing demand for food in the 18th and 19th centuries and how farmers might have tried to produce more food.
- Imagine it is c. 1790. They are journalists writing an article on improvements in animal breeding. In their article they should include interviews with Robert Bakewell and butchers from Smithfield Market.
- Role play an enclosure meeting or stage a debate on enclosure. What were the most powerful arguments in favour of enclosure? What were the most powerful arguments against enclosure?
- Write a letter of protest from 'Captain Swing'.
- Write what the prosecution barrister might have said in his summing up speech against the Tolpuddle Martyrs. What might the defence barrister have said in their favour?
- Imagine it is c. 1850. They have been given a job selling new machines to farmers who still use old methods. They must make a presentation showing how farming techniques are changing and how these changes are improving farming. They must also explain why it is worthwhile for the farmers to buy the new (and expensive) machines.
- Pay imaginary visits to a village in 1750 and again in 1900. They have to describe and explain the main changes which have occurred.

The transport revolution

There are good opportunities here for a local study and for visits to local sites. Canals are particularly worth visiting, especially when there are plenty of original features left (for example, locks, bridges, aqueducts, basins, warehouses).

Less specific activities include:

- Pupils imagining they have just travelled by coach in the mid-18th century. They are so disgusted with the journey that they write a letter to the coach company to complain. What might they have said?
- Designing advertising posters for the roads of Metcalf, Telford and McAdam.
- Deciding where and how to build a turnpike road (see John Nichol's *Developing Britain* for a good case study).
- Designing and writing a brochure encouraging people to invest in a new turnpike trust, canal or railway company. They must explain why the money is needed, what it will be spent on, and why people should invest.
- Playing an IT canal simulation. *Canal Builder* (AVP) is set in the 1790s. Pupils must cheaply construct a canal between two towns which carries as many profitable goods as possible. On completion, the program comments on the merits of the chosen canal and gives a score. *Canal Building* (King's College/AVP) puts pupils in the role of canal builders. It starts with a screen map of NW England in 1770 showing early navigations. During the next 50 years, rival companies aim to build canals across the Pennines to link the growing textile and mining towns of Lancashire and Yorkshire with outlets to the coast. Pupils can compare their results with three canals eventually built across the Pennines and with the many other abortive schemes proposed during the period.
- Imagining they saw Trevithick's steam engine at Euston in London in 1808. They describe what they saw, heard and smelled. How important do they think that this development might be for the future?
- Designing a poster advertising an early locomotive to convince coal mine owners to invest in it.
- Writing a letter to a newspaper commenting on the opening of the Liverpool-Manchester railway. Or half the class might write speeches in favour of the coming of the railways. The other half write speeches against railways.
- Designing the front page of a newspaper in October 1829 which has as its major story the 'Rocket' winning the Rainhill trials.
- John Nichol (in *The Industrial Revolution*) has a game, 'Railway Developer' which is designed to help pupils see what planning a railway might have been like. The game is for two players and the aim is to make the most money. There is a 'board' and the players have to decide where to build their railway lines. The important thing is to get their lines to towns and coal mining areas before their opponent. Pupils must keep an account of their income. Nichol also suggests they keep a diary

of their plans: why they are building the railway in a particular way and what happens as the railway is being built?

The industrial revolution

There is tremendous potential for all kinds of local study. We have concentrated on textiles, coal, and iron and steel but you might look at shipbuilding, pottery, the chemical industry, machine tools, etc. Much depends on the part of the country in which your school is based.

In general terms pupils might:

- Brainstorm what they think the industrial revolution might have been about. What kinds of things would they expect to happen in a country having an industrial revolution? What might need to happen to bring about an industrial revolution? How might it change people's lives?
- Discuss the advantages and disadvantages of the domestic system.
- Play John Nichol's 'The Envelope Factory' (found in both *Developing Britain* and *The Industrial Revolution*). Pupils are members of a team which has to make envelopes from sheets of paper. Each team is judged on how many envelopes it makes in five minutes and how good the envelopes are. The idea is that the teams which use specialisation of labour should win hands down. This should give the pupils some understanding of why the factory system replaced the domestic system and what it was like.
- Imagine they are visitors to Cromford in the late 18th century. They describe everything they see.
- Write an obituary of Richard Arkwright.
- Play John Nichol's simulation 'Cotton Master' (in *Developing Britain*). First it is 1782 and pupils have to decide where to build a cotton spinning mill. It is then 1790 and pupils have to decide how much cloth to make in the coming year. (There is plenty of information to help them.) The scenario moves on to 1845. Pupils are given a map and have to plan their own cotton town, drawing on a number of features to a scale which they are given. Nichol suggests that for each of the tasks pupils should keep a diary, giving in full the reasons for each of their choices/decisions.
- Design a time chart to show the main developments in steam power in the 18th and 19th centuries.
- Imagine they are interviewing James Watt towards the end of his life. What questions might they ask him? How would Watt have replied?
- Design an advert for one of the great inventions in the textile industry: the Spinning Jenny; the Spinning Frame; the Spinning Mule; the Power Loom. Different groups could do different adverts.

- Write an imaginary letter of protest from 'Ned Ludd'.
- Suppose they are interviewing hand loom weavers in 1800, 1820 and 1850. What might they have to say about the impact of steam power at these dates on
  - cotton spinning and factories
  - cotton weaving
  - work and income
  - family life?

- Construct a timeline of the *main* developments in the iron and steel industry in the period.
- Keep a diary as if they were spending a day on work experience at an iron works in the late 18th century.
- Examine the famous picture of Coalbrookdale in 1758 (it is in virtually every textbook) for clues about the making of iron. What can they see? What can they infer?
- Write an obituary of John Wilkinson or Abraham Darby.
- Imagine they are guides taking tourists around an iron works in the mid-19th century. What might the tourists see, hear and smell? How has the making of iron changed over the last 50 or 60 years?
- Discuss in groups what factors might have helped increase coal mining output in the 18th and 19th centuries.

Working conditions

This is an important topic which is generally enjoyed by pupils. The following are possible activities:

- Give pupils visual and written evidence of working in coal mines in the early 19th century. From the evidence, they have to describe what life was like in a coal mine.
- Divide the class into the following groups: male coal miners, female coal workers; child coal workers; coal mine owners; members of an investigative Commission of Inquiry. Each group is given information about its role. The Commission of Inquiry hears the evidence, questions the witnesses and makes a decision about what should be done. It is worth using the video camera to record the proceedings of the Commission.
- Group discussion on why parents were so keen to get their children jobs in cotton mills in the early 19th century.
- Pupils imagine they are a reporter writing a news story about working conditions in a cotton mill in the early 19th century. They may interview anyone they wish. They must decide who they would interview and what questions they would ask.

- Pupils draw two columns, one headed 'Mill' and the other headed 'Mine'. They are given a variety of sources and have to list the problems associated with working in mills and mines in the early 19th century. They conclude by saying whether they would have preferred to have worked in a mine or a mill – and why.
- Pupils write an imaginary speech by an MP in favour of children being allowed to work in mills, mines and factories.
- Play 'Jackson's Mill' in Tim Wood's *Playback: History Roleplays*. The year is 1830. Pupils are a group of important MPs trying to help Lord Shaftesbury. They examine five witnesses who work at Jackson's Mill in Manchester and look at other written and visual evidence.

Industrial towns

Pupils might:

- Imagine they have paid a visit to a rapidly expanding industrial town in the mid-19th century. What would they have seen, heard and smelled. They visit a poor person's house. What was it like?
- Draw up two columns. In one column they list evidence that convinces them that life was getting better in the early 19th century. In the other column they list the evidence that convinces them that life was getting worse.
- Produce a report on the living conditions of the poor in an industrial town in the mid-19th century. What might they say about streets and sewers, housing conditions, diseases, and death rates? What suggestions would they make about how to improve conditions?
- Work out the rules they would impose in their ideal workhouse.
- Play the 'Westford Workhouse' role play in Tim Wood's *Playback*. The year is 1842. The pupils are members of the Board of Guardians which runs a workhouse in the Wesford Union. They are meeting to review the situation in the workhouse and to interview three married couples for the jobs of Master and Matron of the workhouse.
- Examine a range of evidence and then decide whether *Oliver Twist* is a reliable source for workhouse conditions. It is worth using parts of either the 1948 film *Oliver Twist* or the 1968 musical *Oliver!*
- Examine primary visual sources from the 19th century depicting women at work and at leisure. What can the pupils infer from these pictures about women's role?

There is a also an important opportunity here for IT work. Microfilms of 19th century census information are often held by major libraries. While learners should see samples of the census returns, they should also search a database constructed from them, investigating the numbers of people in houses, their work, average ages, changes occurring between 1851 and 1891, and so on.

Political developments

Most pupils seem to find this topic dull. We suggest that many of the developments be covered superficially – but do think that a few events, Peterloo and the 1832 Reform Act, for example, are worth a little more attention. Local developments can also arouse interest. If the Chartists were active in your area they are worth studying in some depth, particularly if there was a local rebellion.

Activities might involve pupils:

- Being given assorted pieces of evidence about the Peterloo Massacre. They have to reach a verdict about what occurred. This could just as easily be done by staging a Commission of Inquiry into the Massacre. Half a dozen pupils play various roles – soldiers, members of the crowd, JPs, radical politicians, etc.
- Writing a TV news bulletin describing the events at Peterloo. It is possible to set up a 'real' newsroom situation and drip-feed items of information, including such things as the weather forecast, events abroad, events elsewhere in Britain.
- Imagining it is 1832. Half the class write a speech defending the unreformed parliamentary system. The other half write a speech attacking the old system and proposing changes.
- Composing a speech which a Chartist leader might have made for a 19th century party political broadcast.
- Supposing it is 1848. Half the class write an article for the *Northern Star* describing the meeting at Kennington Common. The other half write an article for *The Times* describing the same meeting.
- Devising their own 'Pupils' Charter' and describing the tactics they might use to persuade the School Governors to introduce the proposed reforms.

Expansion of trade

Thankfully this topic includes the slave trade, otherwise it would be a swine to teach. We recommend that a fair amount of time is spent on the slave trade.

Pupils might:

- Compile a log of an 18th century slave ship.
- Design a poster advertising slaves for sale in the West Indies or the USA.
- Write a short speech against the slave trade or a publicity leaflet for the

anti-slavery movement. What might the supporters of the slave trade have said in response? There is the opportunity for a debate or a Question Time format here.

- Be given trade statistics from important ports, for example Bristol or Liverpool, showing figures for trade in the early and late 19th century. They have to compare the figures and try to explain them.
- Imagine they are British manufacturers in the 19th century. Why would they be keen to keep the cost of shipping very low and why might they have supported the building of steam and iron ships?
- Design a poster advertising one of Brunel's great ships.
- Imagine they are writing a diary entry in August 1851. They have just visited the Great Exhibition on their first journey to London and their first journey by train. What did they see, smell, hear, feel and do?
- In groups devise a TV advert for the Great Exhibition. The result is recorded on video camera.

The American War of Independence

This is an important topic: in many ways far more important to Britain and the world than the French Revolution. There is a host of potentially good stories: the Boston Tea Party, Lexington and Concord, the career of George Washington, for example, but we have always found it hard to teach as well as we would wish – and one of us likes to think he is an American history expert. The heart of the problem is that it needs a lot of time to get the best from it.

Pupils might:

- Write an American petition to Britain in the early 1770s listing American grievances.
- Design the front page of a British or American newspaper giving details of the Boston Tea Party.
- Discuss in groups what the British government should do after the Boston Tea Party. What advice would they give to Lord North?
- Discuss the strengths and weaknesses of the Americans and the British in 1775. Which side seemed to have the greatest strengths and why?
- Discuss the reasons why the Americans won and the British lost the American War of Independence. Did the Americans win or the British lose the war?

The French Revolution and the Napoleonic Wars

The French Revolution is a terribly difficult topic to teach and since this unit is essentially Anglocentric, we suggest that events in France are dealt with superficially – by story, short video and timeline. A reasonable summing up activity might be to get pupils to imagine they are providing a British radio commentary of the execution of Louis XVI in 1793. Contemporary accounts of the execution are not difficult to find. The Revolutionary and Napoleonic wars might also be studied superficially, but there is a place for in-depth treatment of conditions in the navy or army (probably not both).

Possibilities include:

- Pupils write a letter home imagining they have recently been press-ganged into the navy during the Napoleonic wars. What are their first impressions of conditions?
- Set up a role play examining conditions in the navy after the 1797 mutinies. Four pupils play the part of Commissioners of Inquiry. The rest of the pupils represent sailors with a variety of viewpoints. What recommendations would the Commissioners make and why?
- Pupils write a diary of a British soldier in the Peninsular War.
- Pupils compose despatches giving details of the battle of Trafalgar and/or Waterloo.

The British Empire

This too we envisage as a relatively short topic looking at general aspects of empire-building. Events in India and/or Africa follow as case studies. In all cases, the moral aspects of these examples of inter-cultural relations need to be kept firmly in mind.

Pupil activities might include:

- Look at the conflicting evidence for the Black Hole of Calcutta and discuss what they think really happened.
- Produce a TV news report on the battle of Plassey.
- Write an obituary for Robert Clive.
- Interview an imaginary British traveller to India in the mid-19th century. What might s/he have had to say about life in India and particularly about Indian customs?
- Interview a number of imaginary Indians – rich and poor. What might they have had to say about British rule in the mid-19th century?
- Design a story board showing the main events of the Indian Mutiny.
- Half the class is given sources which suggest that the Indian mutineers had good reasons for their mutiny and which generally defend their actions while condemning British reprisals. The other half of the class is given sources which condemn the mutiny, condemn the actions of the mutineers and generally justify British reprisals. Groups are now formed so that half the members have a pro-Indian viewpoint and half a

pro-British viewpoint. Groups have to decide who was most to blame for what happened.

- Map-work tasks showing how Britain succeeded in taking over large parts of Africa.
- Group discussion on why Britain was interested in taking over large parts of Africa. What were the main two reasons?
- Interviewing a number of imaginary Africans in the late 19th century. What might their views on British rule have been? Would they have welcomed or opposed British rule?
- Produce a newspaper account of what happened at Rorke's Drift after seeing extracts from the film *Zulu*. The same task could be set on Isandhlwana after pupils have seen clips from the less good film *Zulu Dawn*.
- Produce either an official British despatch recording the events of the Zulu War or write an account of the war from the point of view of the Zulus.
- Write an obituary of Cecil Rhodes.
- Discuss in groups whether British rule in India or Africa was a good or a bad thing. This can be broadened into a balance sheet for the whole British empire. What were the gains and losses as far as Britain was concerned from having such a large empire?
- Group discussion of the factors likely to have led to the growth of empire. What do the groups consider to be the most important three factors?
- Writing a diary of someone who emigrated to Australia in the mid-19th century.
- Designing a poster aimed at persuading people to emigrate to Australia, Canada, New Zealand or the USA in the mid-19th century.

Ireland and Britain

This is a topic which is unlikely to get much coverage on the British side of the Irish Sea. A pity, because it has much to offer and has considerable contemporary significance.

Pupils might:

- List the grievances that many Irish had in the late 18th and/or early 19th century. How might a British MP have justified British rule in Ireland?
- Role play a Commission of Inquiry set up to investigate the Irish potato famine. Articulate pupils will need to play characters giving evidence to the Commission.
- Conduct imaginary interviews with people leaving Ireland for the USA or Britain in the mid-19th century.

- Produce two posters: one for an Irish group supporting Home Rule, the other supporting the view that Ireland should remain part of the United Kingdom.
- Conduct an imaginary interview with William Gladstone about his plans for Irish Home Rule.

19th century life

Most of the activities suggested for Tudor life could be re-worked for the 19th century, always bearing in mind the greatly improved availability of primary sources. Pupils, whether individually or in groups, could produce a project on a person or an aspect of 19th century life not covered in depth during the course. Projects on aspects of life might include the church, temperance, sport, entertainment, leisure and holidays, law and order, health, domestic service, education, invention, village life, or the Crimean War. Projects on people might include William Morris, William Booth, Elizabeth Fry, Isambard Kingdom Brunel, George Stephenson, Florence Nightingale, Joseph Lister, Michael Faraday, Queen Victoria or Prince Albert, General Gordon, Elizabeth Garrett Anderson, Charles Dickens, W.G. Grace, William Gladstone, Benjamin Disraeli, Kier Hardie, Charles Darwin, Alfred Tennyson, David Livingstone, Mary Seacole, Samuel Smiles. Purchase of the *Changing Times* CD-ROM would certainly help project work. Using selected articles, photographs and illustrations from *The Times* and *The Sunday Times* newspapers over the period 1785 to 1985, the disk gives pupils an insight into the way events were viewed and reported. It contains over 15,000 original reports and over 1,000 photos and illustrations, all of which can be printed. A unique resource.

We suggest that these projects might lead to a display on the 19th century – set out as it would be in a primary school – with attention to presentation and layout and with main points boldly made.

Conclusion

Groups should decide what things had changed and what things had stayed much the same between 1750 and 1900. What do they see as the main changes in the period? Which topics have they most enjoyed and why?

114

The twentieth century world

Overview

This new unit has grown out of the previous unit 'The Era of the Second World War'. One major criticism of that unit was that it was too precisely focused. Given that compulsory Key Stage 4 history is no more and that many – indeed most – pupils will drop history at 14, it makes sense to provide children with a more balanced 20th century perspective. The new study unit says that pupils should be taught in outline about the following:

- The First World War and its consequences;
- The Second World War, including the Holocaust and the dropping of the atomic bomb;
- The legacy of the Second World War for Britain and the world.

Pupils should have opportunities to study in depth at least one related topic, for example, the Western Front; the Russian Revolution; the Depression and New Deal in the USA; the rise of National Socialism in Germany; the role of an individual such as Churchill, Hitler, Stalin, Mussolini, Roosevelt or Gandhi; the changing role and status of women; the Welfare State; the origins of the United Nations, including the UN Charter and the Universal Declaration of Human Rights; the break-up of the overseas empires of European countries; the origins of the Cold War; changes in the arts or architecture.

There are a few comments we wish to make.

1. The prescribed content for this unit is particularly thin. The proposals thus allow teachers considerable freedom. The topics which might be studied in depth could be seen as a scheme of work but should not be read that way.

2. Most pupils who opt to take GCSE history study the Modern World. Some 'Modern World' schools may decide they will achieve better results if they replicate topics in Y9 and at GCSE. We would oppose such cynicism. We think such tactics would be wrong in principal and we suspect that they might also fail in practice. Our experience suggests that students are usually better motivated and often achieve better results if they come fresh to a topic. Therefore we suggest that teachers cover superficially those topics which they know are going to be covered in depth at GCSE. That said, topics such as the Nazis and the Second World War tend to be popular and as such are good ways of advertising Modern World GCSE history. This is an important consideration, given that history teachers do need to win the hearts and minds of Y9 pupils so that

they will opt for history at GCSE. Thankfully there are plenty of other good topics in the new unit. It will be an unfortunate pupil who is obliged to spend long on 'The Origins of the United Nations, including the UN Charter and the Universal Declaration of Human Rights'!

3. Our suggestions for this unit are aimed at Y9 pupils, but much of what we say applies to GCSE work as well.

4. Key questions for the 20th century world are likely to be of the following type:

   – What was the situation in Britain (and Europe) in 1914? How and why had the situation changed 60, 70 or 80 years later?
   – What has been the impact of the two World Wars? Why did they occur? What were they like? What effect did they have?

Introducing the unit

Possibilities include:

● Pupils brainstorm what they know about Britain in the 20th century and try to produce a timeline of the main events.

● They discuss what types of sources might be available for studying the period. They go on to examine examples of types of sources and consider their strengths and weaknesses.

● Show pupils maps of the world and Europe in 1900. Compare these maps with maps today. Ask the pupils to highlight the main changes which have occurred.

● Give pupils photographs of street scenes 1900–14. Ask them to compare the situation then with the situation now. What things are the same? What things are different?

Britain 1900–1914

Learners will have some awareness of how Britain developed in the 19th century. The main emphasis of this topic is likely to be the difference in lifestyle between rich and poor and between men and women. There are many ways in which pupils can tackle these issues:

● They are given various written and visual sources and have to produce a three column diagram showing different aspects of rich, middle class and poor life styles pre-1914.

● They suppose that they are Rowntree surveying poverty in York or some other town. What might a survey have reported about the health, education, housing, food, leisure activities and work of the poor?

● Groups discuss possible Suffragette tactics aimed at winning the right to vote. Would they adopt militant or moderate tactics? If they adopted militant tactics what kinds of things might they do?

- Half the class designs posters or leaflets encouraging women to join the Suffragettes. The other half designs posters or leaflets critical of the Suffragettes.
- Pupils write a diary of a militant Suffragette who has been imprisoned, gone on hunger strike and been force-fed.

The First World War

This topic has great potential. The questions examined are likely to include:

- Why did it start?
- What was it like for those directly involved in the fighting, especially on the Western Front, and for civilians, old and young, male and female?
- Why did the allies win?
- What were the main results of the war?

A reasonable way to start this topic is to visit a local war memorial – or get the pupils to visit one as a homework exercise. They are pieces of historical evidence and can be an ideal focus for a locally based project. There are plenty of possible questions that pupils might be asked to answer. For example:

- How many local people died in World War I and World War 2? (Be careful – how much can we deduce from any one memorial?)
- Do any surnames appear more than once? Which?
- Does the memorial give the ranks of those who died?
- In which branch of armed forces did most of the men serve? (Is this made clear?)
- Does the memorial contain any names of women? Why are there so few?
- Does the memorial have any writing on it apart from the names of the dead? What does it say? Why? Where is the writing?
- Does the memorial take the form of a monument or a simple plaque?
- What is the design of the memorial like?
- What do the pupils think was the function of the memorial? To act as a reminder? To provide a focus for grief? To indicate efforts and achievements of people? To thank God?
- Do inscriptions indicate what one should feel, think, remember?
- Does the memorial show any sign of damage or deterioration? Has it been repaired recently?
- What does the memorial tell you about how the local area was affected by the war?

● What other sources might tell you about the effects of war on the local area? Which of these sources would you expect to be most useful?

We would not spend long on the long-term causes of the war. The events of June-August 1914 are far more interesting. The story of Franz Ferdinand's assassination at Sarajevo is a classic. The Schlieffen Plan and A.J.P. Taylor's 'railway timetable' thesis are also worthy of attention. Pupils could be asked to devise a flowchart showing the preconditions, precipitants and triggers which led to war. Another good activity is to set up groups representing Germany, Austria-Hungary, Russia, France, Britain and Serbia. Each group/country has to prepare to defend itself against the charge that it was most to blame for starting the war. Each group is also given the task of prosecuting, by cross-examination, one of the other groups/countries. At the end pupils vote on which country they think was most responsible for causing the war.

The Western Front is a topic that can be tackled in a host of different ways. Much will depend on school resources.

● Visits to the Imperial War Museum – or to Belgium/Northern France – are definitely worth considering.
● Schools should certainly try to get on video: *All Quiet on the Western Front* (1930), *Oh! What a Lovely War* (1969) and the last series of *Blackadder* (!)

Two IT programs are worth purchasing. *Attack on the Somme* (Tressell Publications) has been successfully used in thousands of classrooms. The 'Introduction' section provides pupils with the types of attacks which could be made on the Western Front. The 'Attack' section involves pupils in the kind of decisions that faced military leaders on the Somme battlefield in 1916. *Battle of the Somme* (Oak Solutions) is a multi-media presentation allowing pupils to explore text, sound, graphics, photographs, databases, maps, laservision stills and movie sequences through a mass of interlinked pathways. Amazing!

Work on the Western Front might involve pupils:

● Designing a trench system and writing a guide to it;
● Keeping a diary of a soldier's experience in 1916 – or writing the ubiquitous letter home;
● Discussing whether 'lions led by donkeys' is a fair summing up of the British army during the war;
● Commenting on the usefulness and reliability of a number of photographs;
● Writing a critical review of the last episode of *Blackadder*.

On the home front, pupils should certainly consider women's role in the war. A letter from a female munitions worker to a soldier in the trenches is something that is rarely done. Pupils might also design a chart – or cartoon strip – to show how women's lives were affected by the war.

The 'conchies' simulation (in Jordan and Wood's *Modern World History*) works well. The class takes on the role of a military tribunal in 1916. The tribunal has to interview four people (each of whom has a character brief) who have applied for exemption from the Military Service Act to decide whether they have genuine reasons of conscience. The tribunal can excuse them if their present job is vital for the war effort. The main question, however, is: are the men genuine conscientious objectors or cowards trying to wriggle out of serving their country?

Why the allies won is still a contentious issue. Groups of pupils can be given various sources offering different explanations for allied victory/German defeat. They then have to rank the reasons and explain why they have placed the reasons in that order.

In terms of examining the results of the war, they might:

- Imagine they are advisors to Lloyd George in November 1918. What advice would they give him with regard to making peace? What should be Britain's main aims?
- Design a table showing the main aims of Britain, the USA, France and Germany in terms of peacemaking in 1918–9.
- Debate whether the Treaty of Versailles was too harsh or too soft? Did the peacemakers do a good job in the circumstances?
- Produce the front page of a German newspaper on 28 June 1919. What might it have said?

Britain in the inter-war period

This is not the most interesting of topics so we recommend that it is dealt with reasonably quickly. The best way might simply be to get pupils to produce a timeline of the main events in Britain 1919–39: political events down one side, economic and social events down the other.

Conceivably, the General Strike could be covered in some depth. Half the class might produce a radio news item giving the Government's view of the first day of the Strike while the other half produce a radio news item giving the TUC's view of events. The two views are then compared. Or get the pupils to imagine they are producing a TV documentary on the General Strike. What would be the emphasis of the programme? Who might they wish to interview?

Life in Britain in the early 1930s can also be a good topic. Pupils might:

- Draw up a list of questions they might like to ask someone who lived in the early 1930s.
- Discuss what the National Government might have done to help the

unemployment situation in the early 1930s.

- Imagine they have been given the job of devising a Means Test. What questions would they wish to have answered?
- Write an article describing the plight of the unemployed.
- Produce a diary of a Jarrow Crusade marcher.
- Discuss whether hunger marches were a good idea. What other methods could the unemployed have used to publicise their plight?
- Divide a page into two columns. One column is headed 'The Hungry 30s': the other 'The Prosperous 30s'. They then list reasons why the 1930s could be seen as both a 'good' and 'bad' decade.
- Discuss/debate whether Britain was generally successful or unsuccessful in dealing with the economic and social problems of the 1930s.
- Work out what industries would have benefited from the growth of the motor industry in the 1930s. What were the likely social effects of the growth of car ownership?

Communism and Fascism

This is an important topic but difficult to teach: it's so vast; it involves a lot of difficult concepts; and it impacts considerably on Modern World GCSE. We suggest departments concentrate on Russia and Italy – although a case can be made for saying something about the Spanish Civil War. Pupils might:

- Produce a diagram showing the main differences between communism and fascism.
- Imagine they are radio or TV news reporters and have been given the job of interviewing Lenin, Stalin or Mussolini. What questions would they wish to ask them? What might their replies have been?
- Discuss whether Stalin or Mussolini were 'good' or 'bad' from the point of view of the effects they had on Russia and Italy. This might be refined by considering the perspective of different Russians or Italians – urban and rural, richer and poorer, men and women.
- Imagine they are one of the millions purged by Stalin in the 1930s. They record what happened to them from the moment they were arrested. Eugene Ginsburg's book, *Into the Whirlwind*, has some vivid descriptions and the film *One Day in the Life of Ivan Denisovich* provides a visual insight into prison conditions in Siberia.
- Write obituaries for Lenin, Stalin and/or Mussolini.
- Devise a cartoon strip to show the main developments in Russia or Italy in the 1930s.

Germany – the rise of Hitler

Hitler still fascinates adults and children to an extraordinary degree. Non-Modern World GCSE schools should spend some time looking at the man and his career. Modern World GCSE schools face a difficult decision: what to cover in Y9 given that Hitler will almost certainly be studied again at GCSE? The best bet might be to give pupils a nibble at Hitler by way of an *hors d' oeuvre* – a tasty morsel before the GCSE feast to come.

Possible activities concerned with Hitler's rise to power include:

- Design a police file for Adolf Hitler in 1923 after the Beer Hall *Putsch*. It should contain a picture, details of his early life, his army record, his character, and his 'crimes'. A 'This is Your Early Life – Adolf Hitler' would work just as well.
- Produce a party political broadcast for the Nazis in 1932. What might have been the response of a liberal or socialist opponent of the Nazis?
- Groups discuss and then rank the reasons why Hitler came to power in Germany in 1933.
- Jordan and Wood have a simulation in *Modern World* of the Nazi rise to power. They outline six fictional characters, representing a cross section of people living in Germany during the period 1919–34. Pupils can take one character and use that person for all the remaining role playing exercises. Answers could be recorded in the form of a diary so there is a 'record' of how the character got on. Alternatively pupils could answer the role playing exercises from the point of view of several of the characters so that they can see the (likely) attitudes and reactions of different kinds of people to Hitler's rise to power. The characters are:
  - A middle class civil servant, working in an Employment Office;
  - A woman who lost her husband in the First World War and who has a job in a grocer's shop;
  - A nurse working in a hospital for wounded and disabled servicemen;
  - A rich industrialist;
  - The owner of a clothes shop in East Prussia who lost a son in the First World War;
  - A mechanic, who is frequently out of work and who usually votes for the communists.

Additional characters might include:

  - An embittered schoolteacher (who was a fighter pilot in the First World War);
  - A rich landowner;
  - A professor at Bonn University;
  - An ex-soldier who believes Germany was stabbed in the back in 1918.

Jordan and Wood's characters, who have quite detailed briefs, are first asked how they might feel about the events of 1919–23. They have to explain any criticisms they might have of the Weimar Government or what they might wish to say in its defence. Would the characters approve or disapprove of Hitler's 25 points? Which would they agree with? Which would they oppose? What would they feel about the activities of the SA? Which characters might have joined the Nazi Party in this early period? The simulation then goes on to examine reactions to events in the later 1920s and early 1930s.

Possible activities concerned with Hitler's actions in power in Germany after 1933 include:

- Groups discuss why there was so little opposition to Hitler in Germany after 1933. (And there was relatively little opposition whatever some – misguided – Marxist historians have suggested.)
- Pupils summarise Hitler's main actions in Germany after 1933 and see if they can categorise them into economic, social, political, educational and racial actions.
- They conduct an imaginary interview with Hitler in 1938, asking him about his policies in Germany since he came to power in 1933. Or they conduct imaginary interviews with a supporter of Hitler and an opponent of Hitler in 1939. What questions might have been asked? What might the answers have been?

The causes of the Second World War

It is difficult to do this topic justice in one or two lessons and yet this is as much time as schools are likely to be able to give to it. For those schools wishing to opt out of the causes of the war a simple timeline showing the main events leading to war will certainly suffice. For those schools wanting to examine the issue in some depth (and we are not sure you should):

- Pupils imagine they are advisers to Neville Chamberlain in 1937. Chamberlain has asked if Hitler is a threat to peace. What is he told and why?
- Groups simulate a Cabinet meeting in Britain in September 1938. Should Britain go to war with Germany over the Sudetenland?
- They discuss/debate whether appeasement was a good or a bad idea.

The Second World War

A much more popular topic. Again much will depend on resources. Schools should try to get videos of episodes of *The World at War* (ITV) and of *Dad's Army* (BBC). Films include *The Battle of Britain* (1969),

Hope and Glory (1987), *Tora, Tora, Tora* (1970), *Memphis Belle* (1990), *The Longest Day* (1962) and *Battle of the Bulge* (1965). And that is just a start.

On the IT front, the PictureBase modules of *The Era of the Second World War* (AVP) include contemporary photographs, posters, maps, documents and text and might be worth buying.

Visits might be made to Eden Camp, Malton, the Imperial War Museum, London, the Cabinet War Rooms, London, and, in concert with the French Department, to the Normandy beaches.

Key questions for this topic might be:

● Why was Germany so successful 1939–41?
● Was 1940–1 Britain's 'finest hour'?
● Why and how did the USSR and the USA join the war?
● Why and how was Germany defeated?

When looking at why Germany was so successful 1939–41, pupils might:

● Design a diagram showing the main features of *blitzkrieg*.
● Produce German and British newspaper headlines for the main events of 1939–40.
● Imagine they are American journalists in 1940. Their task is to explain German success. They can interview German generals, ordinary German soldiers or British or French prisoners of war. GCSE pupils might take these roles.
● Sequence a collection of war photographs from the period 1939–41.

When looking at whether 1940–1 was Britain's 'finest hour', pupils might:

● Conduct imaginary interviews with British soldiers rescued from Dunkirk.
● Devise a Nazi file on Winston Churchill.
● Write an appropriate speech for Churchill in July 1940. (This can be compared with a real Churchill speech.)
● In groups discuss what preparations Britain should make in readiness for a German invasion.
● Interview someone who was alive during the Second World War. The questions and interviewing methods need to be prepared in advance. There is a case for using a questionnaire format, which allows data from all interviewees to be pooled and analysed, showing the range of experiences and views about the war.
● Suppose they are a German spy in Britain in 1940. What kind of report might they have sent to Hitler?
● Write diary extracts for an RAF pilot over the summer and autumn of 1940.

- Discuss (in groups) what might have happened if the Nazis had occupied Britain in 1940.
- Study a number of Home Front photographs. Which might be censored by the British Government and why? They have to write a caption to go with each of the photographs.
- Design posters persuading people to support the war effort. (Show pupils the real thing before or after.)
- Discuss whether Britain should have made peace with Germany in 1940–1.
- Imagine they are giving a radio report in America on the effects of the Blitz on Britain. They have been allocated only one minute. What might be said?

In examining why and how Russia and the USA became involved in the war, pupils might:

- Imagine they are Hitler addressing his senior generals immediately before Operation Barbarossa. What might he have said?
- Discuss Japanese foreign policy alternatives in 1940–1. What would groups have advised the Japanese government to do?
- Devise a cartoon strip to show the main events of the war in 1941.
- Imagine they are writing a report to President Roosevelt giving details of the attack on Pearl Harbour.

In examining how and why Germany was defeated, pupils might:

- Compose an official despatch recording the events of El Alamein or Stalingrad.
- Tape or write a report from the Normandy beaches in 1944 as though they are a BBC war reporter. They might wish to interview Eisenhower, Montgomery, an ordinary British soldier, a German POW, or a French resistance fighter. Again, older pupils might take these roles.
- Discuss (in groups) what targets British bombers should aim to hit in Germany and place them in order of importance. Was Britain right or wrong to bomb towns like Dresden?
- Be given a list of possible reasons why the allies won the Second World War, for example, Hitler's mistakes, Japan's mistakes, British grit, Russian strength, American strength, Winston Churchill. Rank them. Can they add any other reasons?
- Write an obituary for Hitler or Roosevelt.

The Holocaust

This is a controversial but essential topic. Visual evidence might well affect some pupils but, in our view, can and should be shown. *Schindler's*

List is a useful video resource. *The World at War* 'Holocaust' programme provides reasonable primary material which is not too horrific. Follow-up activities might include:

● Pupils imagine they are survivors from Auschwitz. They describe their wartime experiences.
● Groups discuss why exactly the holocaust occurred. Was it inevitable? Should Hitler alone be blamed? To what extent were the German people to blame? Who else should be blamed?

The dropping of the atomic bomb

An important topic which works well. Pupils might:

● Design the front page of an American or British newspaper in August 1945 reporting the dropping of the atomic bomb on Hiroshima.
● Imagine they are producing a TV documentary on the dropping of the first atomic bomb. Who might they wish to interview? What questions would they wish to ask? What responses might they get to their questions?
● In groups be given different sets of sources. They have to examine these and then report back to the class. One set of sources indicates that the allies were wrong to drop the bomb. Another set indicates they were correct to do so. A general debate/discussion follows.

The results of the Second World War

This topic is likely to be covered quickly – if at all. Many teachers, however conscientious, will find it hard to get much beyond 1945 when teaching this unit. There are so many good topics along the way. For those who do make it this far:

● Pupils might design a poster to illustrate the main ideas of the United Nations Charter or devise a Declaration of Human Rights.
● The world after 1945 was very different from the way it had been in 1939. Some of the things that changed were:
  – Germany was divided;
  – Eastern Europe was under Russian occupation;
  – Western European countries were greatly weakened by the war;
  – Russia was now a Superpower;
  – Fascism was defeated;
  – Communism was stronger;
  – The USA now played a leading role in world affairs;
  – Britain lost much of its power;
  – The United Nations came into being;

– The USA, the USSR and Britain soon developed an atom bomb.

Which of these changes do pupils approve of? Which do they think were bad? Which do they rate as the two main changes?

Post-war Britain

We suggest that teachers get individuals or groups to produce a local archive on Britain or the British Empire in the late 1940s, 1950s or 1960s. The pupils need to be told that an archive is a collection of documents, photographs, objects and books from a particular historical time. The material collected is to be displayed and explained to the rest of the class. The archive could be general or on a political topic (for example, the coming of the Welfare State, nationalisation, Clement Attlee, Winston Churchill, Suez, Harold Macmillan, Harold Wilson, Indian independence, or developments in Africa). It could address a social topic, for example music, radio, television, sport, dances, fashion, food, transport, houses, law and order, education, farming, cinema, immigration to Britain, the role of women, etc. Alternatively, pupils may wish to research the story of one town or village or one family or one person during a decade or more since 1945. Pupils should be encouraged to visit their local museum or library and to interview people. Implicit in this is the idea of a class museum, which might focus on just one decade. Parents, the local community, teaching colleagues and the local museum service/records office will all often contribute material. Also, many museums provide excellent examples of how to present archival and artefactual material in order to give a picture of the recent past. There is no reason why parents and local dignitaries should not be invited in for the morning or afternoon when the material is to be displayed.

Conclusion

Conclude the unit in the same way as the other units but make opportunities to link the history to the present, making the point (which we develop in Chapter 6) that the past is in the present.

CHAPTER 5

Active Assessment

Assessment and learning

A year 9 learner had to do a project on the industrial revolution. The project was partly word-processed, included charts and illustrations and was some 5000 words long. It was essentially a well-written compilation from text and reference books, and included a contents page and bibliography. The comment was:

Introduction and conclusion	7
Graphics	4
Reference	4
Presentation	8
Theme	14
	37/50

A very well produced project with some imaginative ideas. You've tended to stray away from the original theme [The Industrial Revolution] a bit. e.g. You should really have included information on Samuel Greg, Robert Blincoe, Edwin Chadwick and the housing of the wealthy. Rather than information on agriculture and transport. (*Sic*).

Projects may be seen as a form of active history, since they can allow learners to work independently, focusing on areas of particular interest to them. But what is clear from this example is that if active history methods are not matched to active assessment techniques then good intentions will be thwarted. The message from this assessment is that history is about collecting information that the teacher sees as important and presenting it neatly. The principles of active history have been obliterated by inappropriate assessment.

Nor is this just a problem from the past. This topic was marked in 1994. Before turning to active assessment in history we need to set out our view of the purposes and forms of assessment.

Assessment purposes and forms

We identify three purposes:

- To provide *summative* data for employers and for entry to further study. GCSEs are the most obvious example of this use of assessment. These data can be very useful to school management, who might analyse them to identify especially effective teachers, or to see whether certain groups of learners – girls, for example – are being well served or held back by their courses.

- For the *formative* purpose of telling learners how well they are doing, what they can do well and what needs further attention. This use of assessment data can also provide motivation for learners, through giving them goals to aim at.

- For the *formative* purpose of telling teachers how well their intentions are working out in practice. Not only can they see how well learners have mastered content, concepts and procedures and adjust their teaching accordingly, they can also use this information to get a better match between the work they set and the learner's level of achievement. Educationists hold that a good match between the learner and the task is important for effective learning and progression, although they recognise that there is a place for tasks that are slightly too hard for learners. 'Optimal mismatch' is seen as an important device for moving learning along, for promoting progression.

The summative dilemma

We have implied that summative assessment comes at the end of a course and sums up learners' achievements. It does not produce data that are then used to improve learners' performances. It usually 'counts', in that the marks awarded matter and we can describe it as 'high status' assessment. Because Standard Assessment Tests (SATs) scores (if SATs for history are ever developed) and GCSE grades are so important for schools and learners, it is important that the procedures used are a fair or valid test of what learners have done. They must also be reliable, which means that quirks of the test or its marking have not had much influence on the final score. GCSE Boards go to considerable lengths to ensure that their summative assessments are reliable and valid, although there is room for argument about how valid they really are and the extent to which the assessment can be reliable. The dilemma is that GCSE and SATs measure the performances of different learners who have been differently taught in different environments, responding to different questions or tasks. However carefully this is done, it will always be flawed to some degree. So, people answering source-based questions on Elizabethan puritanism face different problems from those faced by people answering questions designed to be very similar but which relate to life on the Great Plains after the American Civil War. The best way of reducing this unreliability is to set learners a whole series of assessments of their understanding, which is not feasible, even were it to be educationally desirable.

This leads to a fairly obvious point that is often overlooked. Assessment is the collection of a sample of evidence from which inferences are made about what the learner knows, understands and can do. It is never objective. Errors are inbuilt. Assessment does not bring certainty, it merely reduces the degree of uncertainty. So much depends on the results of summative assessment, but it is often forgotten how intrinsically flawed is *all* assessment.

Nor can we share the view of some teachers in the recent arguments about SATs, that summative assessment by teachers is preferable to summative assessment by outside agencies. Indeed, teachers can set work that is better related to the slant of the curriculum that learners have followed, but there is no reason to believe that this is a more accurate estimation of learning than one done by outsiders, and some reason to believe that it might be a poorer estimate.

Formative assessment

Formative assessment *informs* subsequent teaching and learning. We would still expect the assessment to be valid but there is not such a pressure for it to be reliable, since the grades do not count in the way that they do with GCSEs. Furthermore, the teacher is able to correct any inaccuracies in the light of subsequent data and apply expert judgement to any odd results. Generally, formative assessment will be 'low status' assessment.

This is somewhat ironic, since we might say that formative assessment is central to learning, whereas summative assessment is central to curriculum management and accountability. Because people react differently, according to whether an assessment is seen as formative or summative, it is hard to use the same assessment for both purposes.

It is a myth, though, that there are some methods that are only appropriate to formative assessment, while others are for summative purposes alone. The difference between the two forms is a difference of purpose and a difference in the treatment of the results, not a difference of method. Mock GCSE examinations are an example of methods that might be called summative being used for formative purposes. However, that is not the same as saying that the same assessment can be used for both formative and summative purposes at the same time. The more we believe a test will count (have a summative purpose), the more we will use every wile, including dishonest ones, to get the best score. However, assessment for learning (formative assessment) depends on an honest appraisal of where more work is needed and we shall argue that self-assessment is often appropriate and desirable.

It will be obvious that formative assessment is more common that summative. The biggest problem with formative data is not so much getting it as having the time to use it effectively. This shortcoming can be reduced if formative assessment has been strategically planned. Suppose that most of the routine assessment is purposeful and that most tasks have a worthwhile and understood learning and assessment purpose behind them. It is quite feasible to mark out one or two tasks in each batch as 'sensitive indicators', ones that will be examined particularly carefully and taken as indicators, for formative purposes, of how well learners can demonstrate key concepts or procedures. The idea is to use that information in the planning of the next topic, so that work can be better matched to individuals' performances and so that problematic points can be deliberately covered, perhaps with a sub-set of the class group.

Routine assessment

It has been implied that there is a third type of assessment, which we will call routine. This is where work is set with no particular goal in mind beyond ensuring that learners are occupied and engaged with the material. The topic that was described at the beginning of this chapter seems to be an example of routine assessment. We do not want to take a 'holier than thou' stance and say that routine assessment is bad – it does keep children engaged and to that extent it is useful for motivational reasons. Besides, setting focused tasks can be demanding and wearisome. Moreover, there is a need to ensure that learners gain a raft of information about a topic before we ask them to interpret, analyse, synthesise or evaluate. We do want to make two points, though. Firstly, it is important that routine assessment does not shut out formative assessment. We do need to know what children know, understand and can do in terms of the attainment target and GCSE criteria, and it is important that some tasks are set to tell us, and to allow us to tune our teaching. Secondly, routine assessment can also use the same methods as summative and formative assessment. Again, the difference is in the purpose of the assessment.

Table 5.1 summarises the different types and purposes of assessment.

Assessment type	Assessment purpose
Summative	Data for certification, management and accountability.
Formative	Data to enable work to be matched to different learners: to help us to tune our teaching.
Routine	No great learning purpose: to engage learners with the material.

Table 5.1 Types and purposes of assessment

Assessment and active history

How does assessment fit with active history?

The methods used for summative assessment are in the hands of the GCSE Boards, who are rightly very concerned with reliability. One of the hardest parts of secondary teaching is learning to apply GCSE standards reliably to the formative assessment of Year 10 and 11 learners. Teachers have a freer rein over the methods used for other purposes and with younger learners, since reliability is not the main issue with formative assessment and hardly considered with routine assessment. Active assessment is as possible as teachers wish in their normal classroom work – certainly in Years 7–9.

Active assessment, active learning

Anything that we do may be assessed. It follows that any of the activities described in Chapter 3 may lead to assessment. Active assessment, then, is when judgements about learning are based more upon 'active' tasks than upon traditional essay-writing activities. Active assessment, it seems, should follow on automatically from active history, but Table 5.2 shows that other outcomes are possible.

	Learning approach – active	Learning approach – traditional
Assessment approach – active	Active assessment.	Unlikely! (although GCSEs may feel like this in a traditional department).
Assessment approach – traditional	Active learning compromised by the assessment programme.	Traditional history – see the topic at the beginning of the chapter.

Table 5.2 Assessment and learning

Implicit in this table is the idea that assessment practices have the power to override the 'official' curriculum and bend an apparently active approach into a more traditional shape. In other words, quality in education comes from the quality of teaching, certainly, and from the quality of curriculum planning as well. But it also depends upon assessment practices being aligned with both, otherwise assessment will produce a 'real' curriculum at variance with the intentions of plans or pedagogy.

This 'assessment backwash' is well known. It can be used to support innovation as the *Schools Council History 13–16 Project* showed. It defined assessment requirements at an early stage and deliberately used the GCE/CSE examinations, convinced that success was only possible if the Project philosophy was worked through into the curriculum. However, where assessment is considered as an afterthought, bolted-on to the curriculum, there is a danger that traditional assessment methods will prevail. These may send messages to the learners that their demands are the ones that matter: that the messages being sponsored in the classroom can safely be ignored.

Active assessment and clear goals

We conclude that it is important that a department planning active history courses needs to pay attention, at the planning stage, to assessment, ensuring that it reinforces the messages embodied in the teaching. Consequently, it is important that not too much of the assessment is routine. There needs to be a significant amount of formative assessment, designed to assess learners' progress towards the goals of active history.

This implies that there exists a set of goals organised in the shape of an account of what progression in history learning might look like. This position is not without problems and these have been well rehearsed by critics of the National Curriculum arrangements for history. In their common refrain that history learning is so distinct that it cannot be analysed in this way, they have not recognised that the same is true of most human learning. Many critics of the old history National Curriculum would be surprised to know that their concerns, usually attributed to history's distinctive nature, are equally applicable to science or to mathematics. For example, it is often said that learning in history is not sequential, in the sense that it cannot be broken down into a series of levels of mastery that succeed one another. It might be said that the same is true of maths, (Dowling and Noss, 1990), so that history is by no means unique in this respect. However, the criticisms made of the ten-point scale used in the old National Curriculum are worth taking seriously. It is debatable whether learning does follow the sequence set out in that National Curriculum, and there are good reasons to suppose that some stages were missed out, while others had little meaning. In part, this reflects the chronic lack of research into the psychology of history learning, but it is also a product of the general intractability of trying to pre-specify the course of learning.

The same can be said of the observation that the old ATs in history were inextricably linked, so that it was a nonsense to suppose that AT2 (interpretations of history) could be assessed apart from AT3 (source handling). Other subjects were in the same boat. It is, as we shall argue, doubtful whether the new, single-AT structure for history deals with a fundamental assessment problem that concepts, skills and information interpenetrate each other. Booth and Husbands, writing of the old National Curriculum for history, claimed that 'the attainment target model is inappropriate for addressing such a human-dilemma or problem-solving conception of history' (1993, p.33).

There is a feeling that the new curriculum model is superior to the 1990 version. But take the statement of attainment for level 6, which requires learners to

> make links between features within and across periods. They examine and are beginning to analyse the reasons for, and results of, events and changes. Pupils describe and are beginning to explain different historical interpretations... Using their knowledge and understanding, they identify and evaluate sources of information which they use critically to reach and support conclusions. They select, organise and deploy relevant information to produce structured work, making appropriate use of dates and terms (SCAA, 1994, p. 16).

Notice that teachers need to disaggregate such statements in order to clarify their key teaching goals – there are around a dozen in this extract alone. Moreover, it is not clear what pupils are to do – what counts as 'begin to explain', 'critically to reach and support conclusions' and 'appropriate use'?

The official line seems to be that these statements of attainment should not be disaggregated like this, but rather used as guidelines when reviewing learners' history work overall, perhaps once or twice a year, to see which level their work 'best fits'. As it stands, this might be seen as disingenuous, sweeping under the carpet the problems of the old statements of attainment, not actually trying to clear them up.

Yet, a positive side may be seen. Given loose, ambiguous and timid guidance such as this, teachers, in the absence of SATs, are forced back on their own professional judgement. The abandonment of the 1990 attempt to pin down the development of historical understanding, thereby prescribing the key goals of history teaching, means that – subject only to the banalities of the new statements of attainment – teachers set their own goals and can assess them as they see fit.

In practice, we suspect that this means that skilled history teachers will do what they did a few years ago, which is to apply the practices and principles of GCSE history to their Years 7–9 teaching.

An objection to this is that it is beyond novice teachers and those who teach history but who have only a slight background in history. That makes it clear that a departmental stance needs to be built up, a departmental view of what the development of understanding looks like. What ensues is a set of departmental criteria, born out of the dictates of promoting progression. Another reason, which we shall develop shortly, is that learners need to know what the criteria for success are. *Implicit* criteria, as we shall argue, are a hindrance to effective learning.

So, departments ought to draw upon the old and the new National Curricula in order to clarify their learning goals for a five year history course. Although it is open to them to draw upon their own collective wisdom, there is much to be said for setting it in the context of officially approved statements, such as the ATs and GCSE criteria. Those criteria should shape active history learning and assessment.

Work on NVQs and GNVQs has shown that clarifying and communicating assessment criteria are the most important parts of fair assessment, whether the evidence of competence is then marked by teachers, other assessors or by the learners themselves. This, it has been argued, considerably reduces the scope for subjectivity, since any assessment has to be done against clear benchmarks.

Practising active assessment

Every learning task can be seen as an opportunity to judge learners' achievements against departmental criteria, although we feel that this should not mean that all – or even the majority – of tasks are used for that purpose. That is not to say, of course, that tasks should not be set for good reasons.

From time to time, teachers will draw upon the evidence of pupil performance in key tasks and try to set this evidence against the global statements of attainment. It is intended that they should do this by exercising professional judgement to gauge which level best describes learners' achievements in the light of that evidence. While we have sympathy with the goal of breaking away from the swarms of judgements which had to be made under the previous version of the National Curriculum, we are not clear that this process will be substantially simpler, nor that it will be reliable.

Where the purposes are summative, unsolved technical problems mean that teachers simply have to follow their own best instincts. One of these problems is that at different times people's performances vary – for example now at level 6, now at level 4 and another time at level 8. This is a demonstration of the well-known fact that tasks which may look the same often make very different demands upon us and that something learned in one context often does not transfer well to another. A complementary problem is raised by the new portmanteau statements of attainment. If we say that a learner is at level 6, does that mean that she can do $a+b+c+d$, or do we mean that she can do most of them, or that she can do $a+b$ and most of the others? What level of performance is needed before we can conclude that a learner 'best fits' level 6 rather than 5, 7 or 4? How many demonstrations of competence at level 6 are needed before we conclude that a learner is at that level?

Over the next few years conventions will undoubtedly emerge on these points, just as they have for GCSE, where experience of the Boards' application of the criteria has made it clear what the criteria mean. This, we suggest, implies that teachers will need to collaborate to reach understandings of the new curriculum. While we have views on these issues, it is not possible to say what the 'right' answers are.

In turning to assessment for formative purposes, we recall that assessment has usually been done by teachers to learners. This is quite sensible, since it is the teachers who plan the learning activities, the teachers who have a view of what constitutes adequate performance and who have sufficient knowledge to make judgements about the work. This is in no way incompatible with active assessment.

However, it is possible to enhance active learning by giving learners greater responsibility for their own assessment, and since the National Curriculum says that learners should become increasingly independent, there is good reason to investigate this possibility. Both peer assessment and self assessment can be used to involve learners in the assessment of learning. The theory is that they learn through having to apply the criteria upon which the curriculum is built in order to assess work. It is sometimes said that to teach is to learn twice. We would want to suggest that to assess is to learn thrice.

The key is in metacognition, that is in making sure that learners know and understand the criteria to be used in marking. Not only is this a necessity for assessment, but it also has the powerful learning function of helping pupils to master the criteria through applying them in a judgemental situation. They thus become clearer about what it means, for example, to use several sources to produce one account. It will involve teachers in some work in translating the criteria that they have derived from their departmental goals into language that the learners can understand, but this is surely a necessity in any case. If criteria are not put into that language, how can they be communicated to learners? How are they expected to learn the criteria, let alone to be aware that they have learned them?

The drawbacks are obvious. Apart from the issue of subjectivity, questions arise about pupils' ability to assess themselves and each other. However, there are reasons to think that the problems are exaggerated when seen in the context of formative assessment. There are reports of Infants being taught to judge their own work, and this is written into Key Stage 2 requirements for technology, science, art and PE. We therefore see no reason why it should not be done with history in KS3 and 4.

With peer assessment a piece of work may be seen, heard or read by several learners. In higher education there is some evidence that students' average judgements of each others' work fall close to tutors' assessments. Since these tutor assessments are not necessarily accurate themselves, the size of the difference between peer-assessed marks and tutors' marks is not enough to cause alarm. The same might be true for secondary school learners, and where the assessment is formative and will lead to discussion about the work, it could be seen as quite acceptable. If not, the teacher might participate as one of the assessors, only bringing her or his marks into play where there appeared to be a significant failure in the peer marking.

There is some small opportunity here for saving teacher time. A far greater gain is that pupils can learn through assessing, and learn not just about history but also to evaluate their own work, becoming more active, independent, self-directed and empowered in the process.

Assessment and differentiation

An unresolved issue is how far teachers should set common tasks for learners in a class, expecting there to be differentiation by outcome (the more able will respond to the same task in a superior way to the less adept). The alternative is to set some learners a task getting at level 5 understanding, others a task tapping level 6 and others level 7 tasks (differentiation by task). The compromise position is the 'stepped task' where level 5 questions form the first part of the task, giving way to level 6 and then level 7 questions.

When it comes to coping, it is easier to devise tasks of the first sort, but they may not engage all of the group and tasks that lead to baffled and disruptive learners do no-one any favours. Moreover, unless pupils are very clear about what the task is driving at, there is a danger that it will underestimate their ability – some who could do well will not understand that a certain type of performance is called for, and will not do themselves justice. So, if we take the logical step of saying that tasks should be devised to find out who can demonstrate competence on one of our criteria – the ability to separate long- and short- term causes, for example – we have moved towards differentiation by task.

What is abundantly clear is that differentiation is not possible unless departments have a developed sense of the various levels of response. The choice between differentiation by outcome, by task and through stepped tasks will be largely dictated by the historically valuable activity which the teacher wants to set the class. In other words, first consider what would be a valuable activity, and then think about ways of presenting it as a task or set of tasks that will profitably engage the range of learners in a class.

Assessment and coping

Where assessment is seen as something 'bolted on', or where there are demands that learners be frequently summatively assessed, then assessment can lead to unbearable pressures on teachers. Nor will the new statements of attainment relieve these pressures. Relief comes from seeing principled teaching and formative assessment as one and the same. The most powerful advice for simultaneously encouraging quality assessment and avoiding intolerable burdens on teachers is to concentrate on choosing sound activities (Chapters 3 and 4) in pursuit of worthwhile historical learning and to let assessment follow on from that. Our belief is that where summative assessment is not a pressing priority, not only is this a feasible strategy but it also opens up the powerful benefits that may come from using self and peer assessment to inform learning.

We return to the tension between active assessment and the demands on teachers' time in the Conclusion.

Quality in active assessment – summary

- Active assessment will tend to be formative in purpose.
- Assessment criteria, derived from the collective professional expertise

of history teachers, are necessary, should be explicit and should be presented in terms that learners can understand.

- Active teaching methods can be used as assessment opportunities: anything that can be imagined as an active assessment method can be used as one.
- Opportunities should be made for peer and self assessment, recognising that this is something that learners will have to be shown how to do.
- Summative assessments are fraught with technical issues; should be infrequent; and for the time being, should draw upon best GCSE practice (Booth *et al.*, 1987).

CHAPTER 6

Active Issues – History and the Whole Curriculum

Reasoning in school history and the whole curriculum

An integrated curriculum

An educationists' dream has been a curriculum that is integrated, so that one part reinforces others, leading not just to cohesive understanding, but also to greater understanding. Various ways of doing this have been tried. General programmes have been devised to increase lateral thinking and creativity, to enhance analytical and reasoning skills, and to improve performance on intelligence tests.

But we have noticed a strong view among psychologists to the effect that reasoning is essentially 'domain specific'. What this means is that the more one knows about an area, the better one is able to reason about it. Thus, being good at scientific thinking is largely dependent upon knowledge of scientific facts, principles and procedures. According to this view, historical reasoning is related to

- the possession of historical knowledge;
- an understanding of the sort of study that history is;
- knowledge of history's skills or procedures.

If children's historical reasoning appears to be less impressive than their mathematical reasoning, the cause might be a lack of sufficient, appropriate teaching.

It is possible to extend this view and argue that the scope for curriculum integration is limited. If thinking is domain specific, what is the point of trying to associate history and science, history and geography, history and English?

In Chapter 2 we argued that the domain specific view is overstated. While reasoning and knowledge of a domain are associated, there is evidence that what we can do with our knowledge is constrained by our general thinking power. There are various neo-Piagetian theories of mental development, all of which recognise that our thinking is the product of general mental structures *and* of specific experience and knowledge. This implies that there is scope for greater curriculum integration, since developments in general reasoning within one subject might have an influence in other subjects.

History and curriculum integration

One of us has argued that subject integration needs to be understood in two senses: integration of content and integration of procedures, or ways of working (Knight, 1993). On such an analysis, history has much to offer the curriculum as a whole. It teaches *content* and *concepts* that are important in their own right and which may well relate usefully to other areas of the curriculum. Its *ways of working* have some distinctiveness, notably the concern for primary sources, interpretation and points of view. However, other subjects are also interested in such things, and other ways of working – collecting evidence, synthesising, analysing, communicating, defending, hypothesising, for example – are common to secondary school work.

We suggest, then, that school history can be analysed into five forms:

1. Topics mainly of interest to history departments – Marco Polo's life, for example. (But the story of the meeting of cultures has implications for the development of inter-cultural understanding.)

2. Topics chosen by history departments but which naturally overlap with topics taught in other departments – local history, for example.

3. General themes and issues, such as environmental awareness, citizenship and economic understanding, which ought to have a historical dimension that is treated with proper historical rigour.

4. Methods that are essentially historical but which may be related to methods used in other subjects. An example of this is 'empathy', something essential to historical enquiry, but also to geography, RE, ME and English.

5. Ways of working that are common to most school work – for example, oral and written communication, planning, working in groups and evaluating.

We are arguing that where school history exists in isolation it may be learned and assessed actively but it is limited through being separated. Where history is seen to permeate learning, both through its concerns and through shared ways of working, it is less open to the charge that it is an inert subject, of little use or relevance and hardly helping to prepare learners for life after school. We are now defining 'active' not just in terms of learning and assessment methods, but also in terms of the potential that history has for being useful.

This is not the same as saying that the only history that should be taught ought to be directly 'useful'. Our claim is that history is useful as a form of enquiry, as an orientation within a culture, and for the insights it can add to other curriculum areas. It is also useful because it teaches ways of enquiry that are similar to the forms of reasoning prized by other subjects. It is useful, then, for its content and associated concepts and for the ways of working embedded within it.

We will develop this argument by examining history and the cross-curricular themes and issues identified by the National Curriculum, before turning to the case of history and the Technical and Vocational Education Initiative (TVEI). We will conclude this chapter by looking at history's ways of working, arguing that history can be taught to encourage metacognition, thereby contributing to learning in general.

Cross-curricular themes – the limitations of a serendipity approach

It has been noticed that the curriculum originally planned for schools in 1987 looks remarkably like that suggested in 1904. If the list of subjects looks well-worn, their content has altered somewhat and there are also the cross-curricular themes and issues to be considered. These do have something of the air of an afterthought, and government reluctance to give guidance on the handling of inter-cultural awareness suggests that there may be some lack of enthusiasm for them. However, the 1988 Education Reform Act makes it quite clear that the National Curriculum is no more than a basic curriculum and that schools need to do much more than cover it if they are to provide an adequate curriculum. We are sharply aware that the demands of the National Curriculum are daunting. Teachers have coped by concentrating on the basic National Curriculum. In the longer term we think that confidence will return and that schools will again explore the possibility of making a whole curriculum with the National Curriculum as its base.

For that to happen, schools aiming to provide a quality curriculum will need to see how the National Curriculum subjects can contribute to themes such as:

- Environmental education
- Education for citizenship
- Economic and industrial understanding
- Understanding of other cultures and ways of life

- Health education
- Careers education and guidance.

It is hard to see that history can do a great deal to help the specific business of career choice. However, quality history work may help learners to see that the job market is changing; that knowledge (in the sense of skills as well as concepts and information) is the hope for future prosperity; that gender roles in work are changing but not fast enough. It may thus do something to make pupils aware of the range of career choice available to them.

The other five themes and issues can and should each have a history dimension. Before discussing this in detail, we want to argue that it is not sufficient to say that history is an active subject because it can be associated with these areas of importance. It is not unknown for teachers to trawl through their syllabi and claim, for example, that history does much to promote economic and industrial understanding because learners find out about trade (in medieval times), about industry (in Victorian times) and about unemployment (in the 1930s). This serendipity approach is deficient on two counts.

Firstly, unless something is done to make learners actively aware of the parallels between *then* and *now*, that is to see that history may have something to contribute to their understanding of trade, industry and unemployment in the present, there is every likelihood of this material being filed as quaint historical data. To use history actively to shape present understandings requires deliberate work to see how far past situations were different as well as similar. In any case, good practice suggests that if we wish to shape ideas about trade, industry or unemployment, we first need to establish what concepts learners bring with them to the classroom (see Chapter 2). Quality history work needs to see an interplay between present concepts and past situations.

Secondly, this is all well and good but rather limited. What message about industry comes from studying the Victorians? Presumably, that industrial work leads to a life that is nasty, brutish and short (managers and capitalists are a different story). Now, we cannot deny the historical accuracy of such a view, vividly expressed by Dickens in *Hard Times*. But is it acceptable to leave it at that, so that children's economic awareness, as developed through history, is shaped only by this gloomy view of the industrial revolution?

We suggest that an active approach to a theme such as industry starts with clarification of what we wish to propose about industry in modern Britain. A school might want learners to be aware that industry takes many forms; that manufacturing industry is rarely sweaty metal-bashing; that skills and knowledge are needed; that men and women both do industrial work, although in many industries (British Rail, for example) tradition enshrines gender inequalities; that industry is vital to the economic well-being of the country; and so on. We might call this a root definition: it sums up the awareness that a school hopes its graduates will take with them.

Working from such a root definition, it is possible to return to the National Curriculum for history and to identify points at which some of these themes might be raised. Not all topics lend themselves to all these ideas, but when we look at a five year curriculum, opportunities can be seen within history for developing awareness of these themes, awareness which will also be developed in other subjects.

In this way, we put thinking about these issues at the heart of planning, instead of engaging in the sophistry of serendipity by saying that we mention service industries when we do the medieval town: history must therefore be responsibly contributing to the whole curriculum! Moreover, learners benefit from the synergy that can arise where different departments are working to similar scripts.

It will be obvious from this discussion that we do not expect that many schools will be able to adopt such a thoughtful approach until the Dearing-reformed curriculum has had a chance to bed down and teachers of all subjects are comfortable with its demands.

History and controversy

Once we move from a mentioning strategy (we told the kids how the Tudors devastated the forest environment of some areas), towards a strategy that still covers Tudor deforestation but in the context of the interplay between people and the environment, we cannot duck the fact that all these issues are deeply controversial and highly political.

Take citizenship education as an example. Government wishes teachers to show how citizenship lays upon us obligations as well as conferring rights upon us. If we treat the trades union movement as anything other than a quaint story about how people got the protection they so richly deserved, we face awkward questions about the present. What of the trades union legislation of the past 15 years? And what rights do we have? With the right to silence being weakened, with trial by jury curbed in Northern Ireland, with the privacy of the ballot box compromised by MI5, and with the British government regularly being overruled by the European Court of Justice, questions about the sense in which the UK is a democracy can hardly be avoided if we take the theme seriously. This is even more the case if we look at the duty that the state might be thought to have towards its weaker members – the old, the poor and the ill. It is a lot easier to fence off into the comfortable confines of the past awkward questions about what it means to be a citizen, as though the Electoral Reform Acts and the Beveridge Report solved the matter.

Implicit in what we are saying is the idea that if history is to be active in the sense that we are now using the word, it will be controversial. Environmental issues, the nature of citizenship, of economic activity, of health care and fairness towards people of whatever sex, religion, class or culture are all deeply controversial matters. If history takes them seriously, as Professor Slater noted (quoting Kruschev), 'historians are dangerous people' (DES, 1985).

History and TVEI

One way in which history can be seen as active is through its contribution to cross-curricular themes that are seen to be important in the education of future citizens. This is essentially integration around content, with historical content contributing to an understanding of wider themes. History may also contribute to the whole curriculum through its procedures.

TVEI put money into schools which orientated their curricula to raise learners' awareness of the world of work and which stressed the skills and knowledge valued by employers. Some historians saw that they could make a strong claim that their ways of working did much to promote such skills. Their departments got resources for doing computer-assisted work on Victorian censuses – something intrinsically valuable in history and entirely compatible with the goals of TVEI. Historians, though, were not as adept at developing this line of activity as were geographers working with the Geographical Association.

What we are driving at is that, whether or not history is organised in the active manner that we described in earlier chapters, it is fostering ways of thinking and working – skills, if you like – that have a value way beyond the history classroom. Furthermore, these are skills that are promoted in other subjects too and which are at the heart of many schools' curriculum development plans.

TVEI did not coerce good history departments into betraying their birthright for a fistful of Nimbuses: TVEI gave money to good history departments because they were able to show that *what they did naturally* happened to be the sort of thing that employers valued. In this sense history has much to offer the whole curriculum. Sometimes, history teachers have not been sufficiently vigorous in making it clear to colleagues, learners, parents and governors how medieval history, for example, could be doing anything more than wasting space that more 'relevant' subjects might be using.

Consider a recent list of the qualities that employers look for in graduates (Harvey, 1994). We think that much the same could be sought of 16 year olds, albeit in a less developed form:

1. Intellectual ability
2. Listening skills
3. Initiative
4. Creativity
5. Team work
6. Explaining skills
7. Oral communication skills
8. Written communication skills
9. Problem-solving skills
10. Innovation
11. Analytic skills
12. Ability to make good judgements
13. Critical thinking skills
14. Interpersonal skills
15. Leadership skills.

Without exaggeration, we might claim that active history should exercise 1, 2, 5–9, 11–13. A case might also be made for the rest. Of course, this is pretty spurious if neither learners nor teachers are aware of having strengthened these attributes.

Integration, metacognition and ways of working in active history

We want to draw together these two ideas – that active history deals with active issues and that it can promote abilities that are actively valued – into a claim that where history is taught actively, as we have suggested, and where it is taught as a coherent part of the whole curriculum, a study exists that has particular power to advance quality education. Naturally, we are not saying that the same is not true of other subjects, simply that active history has more to offer than 'supine' history.

We suggest that history's defence against charges that it is propaganda lies in its ways of working. Some years ago, one of us argued that history is a deeply moral activity in two senses (Knight, 1987b). One sense is that it deals with matters which cannot fail to be moral, since its material is people, their beliefs, choices and actions. The cross-curricular issues that we have mentioned are a particularly lively set of these matters. The other sense in which history is seen as a moral activity is procedural. History teaches that certain procedures are *better* than others: that a preference for evidence is superior to a reliance on cant and conviction; that taking account of awkward information is better than ignoring it; that people, however different they might be from us, need to be understood as people trying to make sensible choices in the situation in which they found themselves; that history's place is to understand rather than to judge.

We suggest that these procedural principles are history's defence against charges that it propagandises when it relates the past and the present through consideration of controversial issues. The conclusions that we may reach about public health provision today may (or may not) be uncomfortable but they are not to be judged according to how comfortable we find them but according to how moral the process of enquiry has been. If it has been intolerant, heedless of evidence, blinkered or driven by conviction, then history has not been active. So far from enriching the curriculum it has diminished it.

Yet, we do not want to rest with the claim that quality history work can address controversial issues in fair ways. We wish to extend the idea and argue that history teaches ways of working that are *generally* useful: locating, synthesising, analysing and evaluating evidence are examples of such skills. A major limitation on their usefulness is that learners often do these things almost subliminally – they are not always clear what it is that they know, understand and can do – with the result that they are not well placed to apply this knowledge to other situations. This phenomenon is often seen in studies of 'transfer of training', where people are asked to apply something learned in one setting to another. Frequently they fail to make the connection and to see that the ability is relevant to the new problem. However, a partial solution is to help learners

- to be clear what it is that they know, understand and can do;
- to think about other circumstances in which this skill or knowledge might be useful;
- to practise consciously applying something learned in one setting to other problems.

So, if we want to argue that history's ways of working have cross-curricular value, it is important to encourage learners to think about the cross-curricular applications of historical thinking. It should not be left to chance.

It is also important for good history learning that pupils be clear about the general principles and procedures they are acquiring. *The Schools Council 13–16 Project* recognised this in its formulation of slogans, such as 'people make history'. Sometimes the slogans were learned but not understood, but we would suggest that this is more promising than the alternative, metacognition-free approach where learners have no understanding of the key ideas and procedures they have been learning.

So, whether the motive is to emphasise the extent to which historical thinking is of value within the whole curriculum, or to improve history learning itself, there is a lot to be said for making learners active in their own learning by making them aware of what they have learned and more thoughtful about how that learning might be applied. The old National Curriculum statements of attainment set out a number of things that learners ought to learn through history, things which are of cross-curricular value, as appropriate to TVEI as to Economic and Industrial awareness, and which learners ought to know that they know and think about applying.

History, we suggest, is active within the curriculum firstly through offering historical insights into important cross-curricular issues and, secondly, through developing ways of working which, when a metacognitive approach is taken, have considerable general educational value.

Conclusion

John Wilmot, Earl of Rochester, once said 'before I got married I had six theories about bringing up children. Now I have six children and no theories'. Like the married John Wilmot, we have some suspicion of educational theory. History should teach its practitioners to beware of heady speculation and to appreciate that theoretical research provides at best tentative generalisations and certainly not 'laws'. Research can do a lot to show some aspects of classroom life but, in the end, so much comes down to the living processes at work in the classroom. No method of teaching works for everybody. Not only are there the unpredictabilities of the classroom, there are also the strengths of the teacher. Just as different footballers have different strengths – a good right or left foot, the ability to head, dribble, pass or tackle – so too teachers have different strengths which they should play to.

However, this is not to say that we cannot learn from other teachers and other classes, or that the general enquiries conducted by educational researchers are of no relevance. But they do not compel us to act in any one way. Rather, they are grist to the mill of professional thought and skilful action. In that spirit, we have argued that history must be taught as an active subject – as one which makes learners active *and interested* participants in the classroom and which is sensitive to the connection between history and live issues that permeate the curriculum as a whole.

Reasonably, it might be said that teachers have much to do just to cope. Learners never seem to get easier to teach, governments never cease to make new demands, and all of this takes place against a backdrop of pressure on schools to improve performance and to cut costs. Yet we reject the view that our suggestions can be treated as 'pie in the sky'. They are designed to promote good history learning. While some of them are undoubtedly demanding and others need some careful thought, all have the power to do just that – to enhance history work.

However, if teachers, one by one, take up some of these ideas, their power will be severely limited – and these educational entrepreneurs will risk 'burn out'. Just as the skilled footballer is necessarily a member of the team, so too teachers do not work in isolation. In recent years a lot of atten-

148

tion has been paid to what makes schools effective and how they might be improved. There is a growing body of evidence that schools do affect children's life chances, that learners with similar achievements on entry to different secondary schools will leave those schools with different qualifications.

Yet, there is a growing realisation that we miss a lot when we focus on the school effect. What about the departmental effect (Smith and Tomlinson, 1991, Siskin, 1994)? Within one school there seem to be more and less effective departments. Departments that are associated with high levels of pupil learning are well managed, not in the sense of being run like petty feudal monarchies, but in the sense of having shared goals and procedures within which each teacher can improvise according to her or his strengths and tastes. The management of secondary school history departments is discussed at length by Brown (1995) and we do not wish to stray too far into that field.

However, there are some things which have to be done on a departmental basis if active learning is to happen and if it is to be as effective as we would wish. For example:

- Goal setting and the formulation of learning criteria – if this is a collective activity, the amount of effort required from each teacher is reduced, in the long run. There are two reasons for this. The most obvious is that this way the learners become familiar with a common way of doing history and so progression can go ahead as smoothly as it ever does in human learning: they do not have to learn new concepts and skills with each new history teacher. Less obvious is the way that this allows planning and development activities to be shared out around the department, so that duplication of effort is minimised. Coping becomes easier if it is collective rather than a case of *sauve qui peut*.
- Assessment – planning a programme of assessment is demanding, especially in the light of the current, deceptively simple National Curriculum requirements. There is a great need for professional development in the field of assessing history learning. Where colleagues work together they can be a resource for each other's learning. More prosaically, the development of assessment activities, levels of response marking schemes and recording practices is beyond most individuals, although there are superheroic teachers who will do it. Lastly, it does no-one any good if this year's learning cannot be organised with some confidence upon the records of last year's achievements. Where assessment is a collective matter, it is more likely that teachers will take each other's assessment judgements at face value, thereby saving their time and reducing stagnation in pupils' learning.
- Liaison with primary schools – this is more fully discussed by Watts

and Grosvenor (1995). Here we simply make the point that the department which is able to achieve curriculum continuity with the bulk of its feeder primary schools is far better placed to provide high quality history learning than departments which have to adopt the 'fresh start' approach with Year 7 learners, almost as if they had no existing grasp of history. While the old National Curriculum was intended to promote such curriculum continuity, the evidence is that secondary and primary schools seldom worked together in order to achieve a mutual understanding of and a trust in each other's methods and standards. This is, of course, a demanding activity and it can only realistically be done on a department-wide basis. Given that KS2 history seems to be working well and appears to be a success story, it is something that needs doing.

There are many other things that also need doing on a departmental basis and which affect the long-term well-being of the department – for example, the induction of new colleagues, collaboration with non-specialist teachers and the supervision of student teachers; the construction and operation of quality assurance systems; and resource provision, including history fieldwork.

Teaching active history is very demanding. No-one should pretend otherwise: quality in education comes at a price and that price is unremitting pressure on teachers and their families. However, intelligent action by departments can provide some relief, especially where innovation and the search for quality are seen as ongoing processes that may be spread over many years.

In that spirit of informed pragmatism, sure of the professional skills, of the intelligence and of the care that distinguish the history teachers with whom we have worked, we commend active history to you – and more particularly, to your department.

References

Aldrich, R. (1984) 'New History: An Historical Perspective', in A. K. Dickinson, P. J. Lee and P. J. Rogers (eds.), *Learning History*. London: Heinemann.

Anderson, L. W. and Burns, R. B. (1989) *Research in Classrooms*. Oxford: Pergamon Press.

Ashby, R. and Lee, P. J. (1987) 'Discussing the evidence', *Teaching History*, 48.

Association of Assistant Masters in Secondary Schools (1950) *The Teaching of History*. Cambridge: Cambridge University Press.

Birt, D. and Nichol, J. (1975) *Games and Simulations in History*. London: Longman.

Booth, M. (1969) *History Betrayed*. London: Longman.

Booth, M. (1979) 'A Longitudinal Study of Cognitive Skills, Concepts and Attitudes of Adolescents...' Reading: unpublished PhD thesis.

Booth, M., Culpin, C. and Macintosh, H. (1987) *Teaching GCSE History*. London: Hodder and Stoughton.

Booth, M. and Husbands, C. (1993) 'The history National Curriculum in England and Wales: assessment of key stage 3', *The Curriculum Journal*, 4(1).

Bourdillon, H. (ed.) (1994) *Teaching History*. Buckingham: The Open University Press/Routledge.

Brown, R. (1995) *Managing the Learning of History*. London: David Fulton Publishers.

Burston, W. H. and Thompson, D. (eds.) (1967) *Studies in the Nature and Teaching of History*. London: Routledge).

Carretero, M. *et al.* (1994) 'Historical knowledge: cognitive and instructional implications', in M. Carretero and J. F. Voss (eds.), *Cognitive and Instructional Processes in History and Social Sciences*. Hillsdale, NJ: LEA.

Collingwood, R. G. (1946) *The Idea of History*. Oxford: Oxford University Press.

Cooper, H. (1992) *The Teaching of History*. London: David Fulton Publishers.

Cuban, L. (1991) 'History of teaching in social studies', in J. P. Shaver (ed.), *Handbook of Research on Social Studies Teaching and Learning*. New York: Macmillan.

DES (1985) *History in the Primary and Secondary Years: an HMI view*. London: HMSO.

DES (1990) *National Curriculum History Working Group Final Report*. London: HMSO.

Dickinson, A. K. and Lee, P. J. (eds.) (1978) *History Teaching and Historical Understanding*. London: Heinemann.

Dickinson, A. K., Lee, P. J. and Rogers P. J. (eds.) (1984) *Learning History*. London: Heinemann.

Dowling, P. and Noss, R. (eds.) (1990) *Mathematics versus the National Curriculum*. Lewes: The Falmer Press.

Doyle, W. (1983) 'Academic work', *Review of Educational Research*, 53(2).

Egan, K. (1979) *Educational Development*. New York: Oxford University Press.

Elliott, G., Sumner, H. and Waplington, A. (1975) *Games and Simulations in the Classroom*. Bristol: Schools Council/ESL.

Fines, J. (ed.) (1983) *Teaching History*. Edinburgh: Holmes McDougall.

Galton, M. and Williamson, J. (1992) *Group-work in the Primary Classroom*. London: Routledge.

Harvey, L. (1994) *Employer Satisfaction*. Birmingham: Quality in Higher Education Project.

Hull, R. (1985) *The Language Gap*. London: Methuen.

Jones, K. (1980) *Simulations: A Handbook for Teachers*. London: Kogan Page.

Joseph, K. (1984) 'Speech to the Historical Association', *The Historian*, 2.

Knight, P. (1987a) 'Children's Understanding of People in the Past'. Lancaster: unpublished PhD thesis.

Knight, P. (1987b) 'Historical values', *Journal of Moral Education*, 16(1).

Knight, P. (1993) *Primary Geography, Primary History*. London: David Fulton Publishers.

Lee, P. J. (1983) 'History teaching and the philosophy of history', *History and Theory, Beiheft 22*.

McIver, V. (ed.) (1982) *Teaching History to Slow-learning Children in Secondary Schools*. Belfast: Queen's College.

Megarry, J. (ed.) (1977) *Aspects of Simulation and Gaming*. London: Kogan Page.

National Curriculum Council (1991) *History Non-Statutory Guidance*. London: HMSO.

NCET (1994) *IT Works: Stimulate to Educate*. London: NCET.

Norman, D. A. (1978) 'Notes towards a complex theory of learning', in A. M. Lesgold *et al.* (eds.), *Cognitive Psychology and Instruction*. New York: Plenum Press.

Oppenheim, W. (1982) 'Complex Games and Simulations in School', *Teaching History*, 34.

Patrick, H. (1988) 'The History curriculum: the teaching of history 1985-1987', *History Resource*, 2(1).

Perret-Clermont, A. (1980) *Social Interaction and Cognitive Development*. London: Academic Press.

Peterson, P. L. (1979) 'Direct instruction reconsidered', in P. L. Peterson and H. J. Wahlberg (eds.), *Research on Teaching*. Berkeley, Ca: McCutcheon.

Pond, M. (1983) 'School history visits and Piagetian theory', *Teaching History*, 37.

Price, M. (1968) 'History in Danger', *History*, 53.

Rogers, P. J. (1984) 'The power of visual presentation', in A. K. Dickinson, P. J. Lee and P. J. Rogers (eds.), *Learning History*. London: Heinemann.

Schools Curriculum and Assessment Authority (1994) *History in the National Curriculum: draft orders*. London: SCAA.

Shemilt, D. (undated) *Adolescent Ideas about Evidence*. Leeds: Trinity and All Saints College.

Shemilt, D. (1980) *History 13-16 Evaluation Study*. Edinburgh: Holmes McDougall.

Shemilt, D. (1984) 'Beauty and the Philosopher: Empathy in history and the classroom', in A. K. Dickinson, P. J. Lee and P. J. Rogers (eds.), *Learning History*. London: Heinemann.

Siskin, L. S. (1994) *Realms of Knowledge: academic departments in secondary schools*. London: The Falmer Press.

Smith, D. J. and Tomlinson, S. (1991) *The School Effect*. London: The Policy Studies Institute.

Smith, L. and Knight, P. (1992) 'Adolescent reasoning tests with history content', *Archives de Psychologie*, 60.

Southern Regional Examination Board (1986) *Empathy in History: from definition to assessment*. Southampton: SREB.

Spartacus Publishers (1988) – news report in *The Times Educational Supplement*, 2.9.88.

Taylor, A. J. P. (1983) 'Fiction in History', in J. Fines (ed.), *Teaching History*. Edinburgh: Holmes McDougall.

Twelker, P (1977) 'Some reflections on the innovation of simulations and gaming', in J. Megarry (ed.) *Aspects of Simulation and Gaming*. London: Kogan Page.

Unstead, R. J. (1956) *Teaching History in the Junior School*. London: A and C Black.

Unwin, R. (1981) *The Visual Dimension in the Study and Teaching of History*. London: The Historical Association.

Watts, D. G. (1972) *The Learning of History*. London: Routledge and Kegan Paul.

Watts, R. and Grosvenor, I. (1995) *Crossing the Key Stages of History*. London: David Fulton Publishers.

West, J. (1981) 'Children's Awareness of the Past'. Keele: unpublished PhD thesis.

Wilson, S. M. and Wineberg, S. S. (1988) 'Peering at history through different lenses', *Teachers' College Record*, 89(4).

Index